CONFLICTING DESIRES

Notes on the Craft of
Writing Erotic Stories

HAN LI THORN

velluminous

Published by Velluminous Press
www.velluminous.com

ISBN-13: 978-1-905605-12-5
ISBN-10: 1-905605-12-9

2 3 4 5 6 7 8 9 10

cover design by Elspeth Fahey

CONFLICTING DESIRES

Notes on the Craft of Writing Erotic Stories

For those who told me when the hammer first rang true
And to those who tell me when it doesn't.

Contents

Introduction

The idea behind this book is that much erotic fiction is astoundingly bad when examined in any terms other than 'hotness'. Many sexy stories (whether published in print, in ebook form, or simply offered for free on the internet) are populated by one-dimensional characters and fueled by hackneyed plots, while the writer appears, too often, to be right there on the page, fobbing the reader off with a knowing wink that says, *'I know this is hack work but hey, there's a really kinky scene coming up and that's what you paid for, right?'*

Truthfully, there's nothing wrong with that approach. Many writers take that path; many readers are happy with the results. Some, however, want more. Some readers are looking for literate, well-plotted works that satisfy more than their libidos. They want erotica, not porn.

Many writers want more, too. I presume that you do, otherwise why would you be interested in this book? Online forums, mailing lists and news groups are also full of evidence of erotic authors wishing to improve their storytelling craft, yet the number of instructional books on the subject is small—and those books often concentrate on selling into established markets that are manifestly focused on something other than quality.

If you've spent any time on Amazon perusing reader-reviews of sexually-oriented fiction, you might be familiar with the occasional expression of delight recorded by a reader who has, unexpectedly, stumbled across a sexy story populated with engaging characters and driven by a credible plot. Perhaps predictably, these reviewers tend to be more than usually articulate. Why should a discerning, intelligent customer be forced to settle for less when reading for arousal than she does when reading for entertainment?

There is a market for quality stories that are both hot and literate. Almost by definition, it's not the mass market, but it exists, it potentially includes everybody who's interested in sex and in good storytelling, and it's not well-served. Erotic writers who can tap that market can sell their work—even if they're not signed with a major trade publisher.

All this begs some questions. Why is there so much mediocre

erotic writing around? How does it get published and why do people buy it? The answers lie both with readers, on the demand side, and with writers, on the supply side:

1. Poorly written, formulaic fiction sells in all genres, not just in the erotic market (many books matching that description also *fail* to sell, but that's a different matter).
2. Sex is a powerful commercial motivator. If a product happens to scratch an urgent erotic itch, it can find a market even if it's not exactly what the customer wanted.
3. Powerful feelings can result in powerful urges to record and communicate those feelings—so it's not surprising that many individuals wish to express their sexuality in story form. Only a fraction of these people have the time or talent to learn how to write well.
4. Even for those who *can* write well, bringing out sexiness and story in the same piece is hard work. Relatively poor erotic writing finds a ready market, so why spend the time and effort on producing the good stuff?

The idea of this book is that it *can* be worth working harder to produce the good stuff, even if it doesn't make strict commercial sense[1]. It's worth doing if you aspire to touch your reader's heart and mind as well as her libido and pocketbook.

It's certainly worth doing if you have any inkling that you might be creating a kind of art.

69

Do you disagree with these ideas? Do you think that the typical quality of today's erotic novel is good enough, so that there's no reason to strive for something better? Do you agree with the chain bookstores that the most important thing about an erotic novel is its cover?[2] If so, then you surely have better things to be doing with your time than reading a book such as this.

---

1   Fiction writing in general seldom makes strict commercial sense. You can almost always make more money doing something else.

2   Erotic editor Mike Bailey tells us that bookstore chains order erotic novels based strictly on cover appeal, rather than on the content or the author's sales record (see Bailey's *Writing Erotic Fiction*, p140).

Still with me? Excellent! What does all this mean to you?

It depends on where you are at the moment, and on where you want to go.

If you're an erotic writer planning to sell novels to the established trade marketplace (to the big publishers who can reliably place their titles in the Erotica section at Barnes and Noble) then this book shouldn't be your first point of reference. My advice would be to obtain and analyze several samples of those publishers' products, in order to understand the style and type of material they can be confident of selling. You can often glean more from their books than from their guidelines (but read the guidelines too, of course). Then come back to this volume to nail things like point-of-view.

If you're a beginner who wishes to learn the nuts and bolts of erotic storytelling craft, then keep reading. As you absorb the information in the rest of this book, you will swiftly shed that 'beginner' status.

If you have some experience, but you're still a bit hazy on ideas such as how classic plots fit into a three act structure, how the various points-of-view work, or what foreshadowing is, then the information in this book can (with careful study) help you raise your literary game.

And if you're already a Mistress (or Master) of the Craft, then my hat is off to you. Now stop wasting your time, find somewhere quiet to sit down, and write an erotic story that's worth reading.

1

Character

The Importance of Character

Erotic stories are stories about human behavior. The genre is fundamental to our nature. Everyone who is here, is here as a result of sex. Everyone who ever will be here (barring cloning and the like) will be here because of sex.

No other area of storytelling can make a corresponding claim. Not science fiction, not crime, not the technothriller, not even romance. Sexual behavior is hard-wired into the human mind because without it, human characters would not exist.

Since sexual feeling is part of being human, it follows that the actors in sexual stories should be human—fully realized, fleshed out characters with whom the reader can empathize and in whom she can believe. Character is at least as important to written erotica as it is to any other genre. You might even say it defines written erotica: lacking character, sexy writing cannot rise above the level of bump-and-grind.

69

Some authors pull characters out of thin air, paying little attention to the process by which it happens. Others observe real people, dissecting their various aspects into the raw material for new creations that are (hopefully) unrecognizable to the originals.

However you populate your stories—even if you're still looking for the method that works for you—it can help to take a step back and spend some time understanding fictional characters from a more analytical viewpoint: in terms of their roles and story functions; their flaws and internal drives.

You will still be able to pull characters out of your subconscious if you wish, or to seek inspiration from life, but you'll also learn how to invent characters from scratch, by considering who you want each character to be. As you gain a deeper understanding of your character's personality and role, you'll develop a clearer idea of the magic you want from her—and of how to extract that magic into your story.

Players and Voyeurs

Every character can act in one of two fundamental roles. The first role belongs to characters whose actions propel the story toward its conclusion. The second role belongs to characters who observe and reflect on behalf of the reader. One character might engage in either role at various times. In this discussion, I will refer to characters filling these two roles as *Players* and *Voyeurs* respectively.

A Player is a character who makes plans and executes them. She decides, acts, speaks, reacts and interacts. Particularly in commercial fiction, the main character is likely to be a Player.

If your story were dramatized for the theatre, the Players would be the ones who, through their words, actions and physical presence, dominate the stage. The terms 'actor' and 'player' have both been used to denote those who bring drama to life on the stage, and for good reason.

The term 'voyeur' derives from the French verb *voir*, meaning 'to watch' or 'to view', and is not used here in its pejorative sense (which is to indicate a person who gets off by spying on the intimate moments of others). Rather, it denotes a character who observes the unfolding narrative and who reports and interprets it for the reader. (In an erotic tale, of course, this observation and interpretation may also trigger a more carnal voyeuristic *frisson*—for the reader, if not for the character).

Although drawn into the Voyeur's mind, the reader does not have to accept his judgements; the Voyeur could be an 'unreliable narrator'. For example, he might be completely narcissistic, seeing only the things he wishes to see and interpreting every event in a way that casts him in the best possible light. Depending on the author's intention and skill, the reader may not accept these perceptions at face value, preferring to rely on the reactions of other characters and on her own insights, all of which might tell a different story.

A character can fulfil the functions of both Player and Voyeur within one scene. Alternatively, a character could move from one role to the other at different times. If you decide that your story can be told without significant reflection on the part of the characters, then you are free to populate it mainly with Players. Taking a story to the other extreme—by eliminating Players—would be more problematic. Without Players, there can be no action and thus no story. A Voyeur, after all, needs something more to observe than the workings of his own mind.

In the wider world of fiction, commercial work tends to be oriented toward characters who act, while literary fiction is often about characters who reflect. Players excel at driving plot, while Voyeurs excel at revealing character.

The balance you strike between the Player and Voyeur aspects will define the kind of erotic stories you create. Sex might be about physical action, but eroticism is more often about the internal lives of the characters, their thoughts and emotions and so on.

Even if you're setting out to write steamy action-driven pieces, you may be able to add another dimension by using a Voyeur in a minor role, or by giving a major Player the occasional scene where she takes some time to observe, reflect, and lay her thoughts bare for the reader.

How Players and Voyeurs Reveal Character

At the simplest level, a character in your story is no more than a participant in that story. At a deeper level, *character* in your story is what you reveal about those participants. This revelation can happen in three ways:

1. Players can reveal their characters through what they do. Every act performed by a character tells the reader something about that character. If a man approaches an attractive stranger and immediately flirts with her, that tells us something about the man.
2. Voyeurs can reveal their characters through introspection and self-examination. A wife watching in bitter silence while her husband flirts with another woman tells the reader something

about the wife's personality, and about the state of their marital relationship.

3. Both Players and Voyeurs can reveal the character of third parties through their judgements and reactions. If a husband flirts with another woman, that tells the reader something about his judgement of her. If his wife shrugs resignedly and lets the matter go, that tells the reader something of her judgement of *him*.

Character Archetypes

If you ever use terms such as 'Hero', 'Villain' and 'Sidekick', then you're already familiar with the idea of specific *kinds* of characters that fill archetypal story roles.

Joseph Campbell's 'Hero's Journey' (discussed further in Chapter 3, *Plot and Structure*, and in Appendix B) includes a large number of archetypes, including (among others) the *Herald, Threshold Guardian, Shadow* and *Trickster*. These archetypes are relevant to the Hero's Journey because they fit the shape of that narrative: the Hero is called to adventure by a Herald, and must pass some test set by a Threshold Guardian before entering the dark world where adventure is to be found, and so on.

These archetypes may sound complex and foreign, but they are not something Campbell pulled out of thin air. They recur again and again in our most powerful myths and stories, everywhere from ancient legend to some of the latest movies that pervade our culture and consciousness. Because of this, it's worth any story-teller having at least a nodding acquaintance with them.

While it would be possible to write a story that included every element of the Hero's Journey, it is usual for writers (and myth makers) to take only what they need—and that is what we will do in this chapter. If you're curious about the bigger picture, please consult Appendix B and the reading list you will find there.

Archetypes are universal. They can be adapted to any kind of story, including erotic ones. The question of purely erotic character archetypes (or more accurately, stereotypes) receives some attention later in this chapter; for now, we'll restrict the discussion to the most fundamental archetypes and their variants:

Protagonist

The protagonist is the extraordinary person whose story this is. Her actions drive the story; her goal is the goal of the story. By the end, the protagonist will have undergone some profound change, either externally (circumstances) or internally (values, belief or outlook) or both. The story may be narrated by the protagonist, or seen through her eyes, but this is not necessarily the case.

In most erotic stories, the protagonist will engage in many sexual encounters throughout the work, but (as ever) there are no hard rules. Imagine a protagonist who remains virginal until her 'profound change' occurs in the last few pages. The eroticism of the tale might arise from the actions of secondary characters, and from the nature of whatever conflict the protagonist faces—and perhaps from her studied emergence from shyness to insatiability.

Hero/Heroine

These terms are often used interchangeably with 'protagonist' but there's more to it than that. In Bret Easton Ellis's disturbing novel *American Psycho*, the protagonist, Patrick Bateman, is presented as a woman-killing sociopath—hardly heroic behavior, yet the story is clearly about Bateman.

A hero is a specific type of protagonist, one who is intrinsically good (if also flawed in some way), and often willing to sacrifice himself for the benefit of others. Beware: if you make your hero or heroine *too* perfect, you will end up with an unbelievable (not to mention irritating) 'Mary Sue' character. We will discuss the need for character flaws later in this chapter.

Antihero

An antihero is a protagonist whose values are in some way opposed to the usual heroic qualities. An antihero might still end up performing good deeds, but they won't come from his heart (unless he achieves some heroic transformation or redemption).

The motivations of an antihero may be selfish, cynical or even cowardly, but that doesn't mean you can't draw him sympathetically, and persuade your audience that he's worth rooting for. A well-drawn antihero will generally be more engaging than an unflawed goody-two-shoes hero.

Antagonist

The antagonist is the embodiment of the forces that oppose the protagonist. Sometimes the antagonist is a person, but it could be a group, a corporation, an animal, a force of nature, or even an object. Even if sentient, the antagonist is not necessarily evil. He may have a perfectly understandable motive to wish to prevent the protagonist from achieving her goals.

You can strengthen your tales by building sympathy and understanding for the antagonist; a work that presents both sides of the story is often more satisfying than a straightforward struggle between good and evil.

Villain

A villain is an antagonist whose motivations are, at best, morally questionable. A villain will never oppose the heroine for the greater good or even for her *own* good; rather he will oppose her for selfish and/or evil reasons. Those reasons must be credible if your reader is to believe in the villain. Few people are motivated purely by the wish to do evil; there is generally something more complex at work.

The line between the antagonist and the villain is not easy to define. Consider a devout parent who rules with a rod of iron, convinced of his moral duty to beat the devil out of his children. In his own mind and to his fellow zealots, his actions are driven by the desire to save souls. To his abused offspring and to the outside world, he may be pure evil.

How will the reader make her judgement? She will rely on her own prejudices and life-experiences, naturally, but she will also respond to the way you present the story.

Sidekick

A sidekick is a close companion and trusted supporter of the main character. In erotic or romantic stories, the sidekick might be a best friend, possibly someone with whom 'nothing could ever happen'—though there's no reason why the protagonist and sidekick shouldn't engage in a little hanky-panky if they're so inclined, and if that's the way the story takes things…

Playmate

The playmate (a term used for characters of either sex and any sexuality) is an object of sexual or romantic desire. Depending on the story, there may be one or several playmates, or none (in a story about a libertine who cares only for flesh without regard for whose flesh it is, the sexual partners will not emerge as developed characters). Naturally, playmates can, in their own turn, desire other playmates.

In many erotic stories, the relationship between the protagonist and playmate may largely be one of unfulfilled desire. In other words, playmates will often be unavailable. The term 'playmate' reflects the protagonist's wishes for this character, which are not always reflected in the character's story-role. If your playmates are always able and willing to hop into the protagonist's bed, you may be missing opportunities for developing erotic tension.

Mentor

The mentor is a wise figure who acts as instructor and guide to the protagonist. In stories based around the Hero's Journey, this is a key role, but its importance is lessened in many erotic tales. Still, the archetype is a powerful one. If your protagonist ever becomes somebody's sexual protégé or trainee, for example, then your story will include the mentor archetype.

Even if you don't have an older and wiser mentor in your tale, you might find that another character such as a sidekick or best friend can provide your protagonist with some welcome insights from time to time.

69

This brings us to the question, 'What are these archetypes for?' A story certainly needs a protagonist and some kind of antagonist, but the remaining archetypes do not necessarily have to be expressed by means of a character. The roles can be omitted, or subsumed into another part.

Imagine an erotic story about two friends who figure as protagonist and antagonist. The protagonist has fallen in lust with his female best friend; his objective is to seduce her. She, in the role of antagonist, throws up one barrier after another but, being his friend, continues to offer support and advice. Perhaps she even tries to help him out by introducing him to some eligible singles from her circle.

The conflict arises from the collision of friendship and desire; the resolution will occur when he succeeds (friendship develops into romance) or fails (the chance for romance is lost; perhaps the friendship is lost too), or some other solution is found.

This story has two main characters, but how many archetypal roles are represented? The man is the protagonist. The woman is his antagonist, but also his sidekick (she does her best to help with his problem) and mentor (she offers advice). Last but not least, she also fills the role of playmate, as the object of his sexual desire.

Don't be misled by the term 'character archetypes' into thinking that these roles must always be fulfilled by human characters. In the erotically-themed movie *Cherry 2000*, the playmate is (initially) a broken sex-android. The protagonist, Sam Treadwell, misses the fun times he had with his android and sets out on a quest to replace it. Being non-human (and non-operational) the android barely qualifies as a character—a fact that helps Treadwell decide which playmate he *really* wants by the end of the movie.

Or imagine a tale about a woman who discovers an ancient erotic text, one that inspires her to embark on a journey of sensual discovery. Isn't the book playing the role of her mentor?

Character Metatypes

The archetypes from the previous section tell you about the story-roles to be filled, but they don't say much about the characters themselves. For a character to live and breathe, he must become more than a simple archetype. He requires underlying drives, motivations and attitudes.

This is where character metatypes come in. A metatype captures some core aspect of the character, providing a skeleton on which you can build. Metatypes work at a high level; they don't try to nail down every detail.

The table opposite lists eight metatypes reflecting the worlds of brawn, brains, power, rebellion, faith, insight, charm and trickery. Each metatype defines some aspect of a character's core persona. A single character can contain more than one aspect.

Metatype	Traits/Motivations	Ultimate Expression Might Be...
Warrior	Strength, Survival, Victory	War heroes, Explorers, Athletes
Scholar	Knowledge, Intellect, Debate	Scientists, Theologists, Philosophers
Hierarch	Status, Privilege, Conformity	Bishops, Bureaucrats, Prison guards
Rebel	Independence, Equality, Individuality	Entrepreneurs, Bohemians, Mavericks
Zealot	Faith, Certainty, Obsession	Evangelists, Campaigners, Stalkers
Empath	Perceptiveness, Insight, Humanity	Counselors, Healers, Artists
Seducer	Glamor, Charisma, Sexuality	Gigolos, Movie stars, Courtesans
Rogue	Guile, Deception, Stealth	Tricksters, Gamblers, Politicians
(Insert any additional metatypes you wish to use in the blank spaces above).		

The list is based on several fundamental wellsprings of character, but you may wish to examine additional metatypes that don't have an obvious home in the basic set. If so, then add them in the space provided—and use them. But bear in mind that a metatype says something about a character's fundamental nature, not what she does or how she feels (though those are vital pieces of information, too). If a characteristic is something that you're going to use directly in your story, then it's probably the consequence of an underlying metatype, rather than being a metatype itself.

Consider a character who plays a sexually submissive role in your story. Where does that submission come from? How about:

- A warrior testing the limits of her endurance?
- A scholar who collects kinky Renaissance art—and acts it out?
- A hierarch craving a clear chain of command?
- A rebel craving an outlet for rebellion?
- An empath taking his understanding nature one step further?
- A seducer turned on as much by her own submission as by its effect on her Master?
- A rogue hoping to be caught and punished?

The answer could be any of the above, or something completely different. In the absence of any answer, however, your character will lack depth. Saying, 'She was just made that way' or 'She happened to meet a dominant man who brought out her submissive side' is not going to satisfy the discerning reader. By identifying a character's metatypes, you build a structure from which credible answers can emerge.

Metatype Pairings

Metatype is a wellspring from which character can flow. It tells you where a character comes from and where he is driven to go. The urges that drive characters can be complementary (reinforcing) or conflicted (opposing).

The eight metatypes in the table fall naturally into four complementary pairs and four conflicted pairs:

Complementary:

- Warrior - Zealot (strength and certainty)
- Scholar - Hierarch (codified knowledge and organization)
- Rebel - Rogue (individualism and dislike of authority)
- Seducer - Empath (love and understanding)

Conflicted:

- Warrior - Scholar (cerebral versus physical)
- Hierarch - Rebel (conformity versus freedom)
- Zealot - Empath (certainty versus understanding).
- Seducer - Rogue (charm versus charm).

Don't be afraid to mix up the metatypes. There's no particular reason for a seducer always to ally with an empath, or for warrior and scholar aspects not to co-exist in a single character. Tension keeps readers interested, whether it comes from your plot or from within your characters. A heroine who is somehow at war with herself will be more compelling than one who is free of any self-doubt.

Archetypes, Metatypes, and Stereotypes
Archetypes and metatypes represent two very different aspects of character:

- Archetype tells us about the role a character will play in the story.
- Metatype gives one or more spines from which we can infer interests, outlook and motivations, and around which we can further flesh-out the character.

You can use a table such as the one shown overleaf to think about the archetype-metatype dimensions of your characters (the assignments in the table are only an example).

In the table, the hero is a warrior and a rebel, while the villain is a hierarch and a zealot, and so on.

	Warrior	Scholar	Hierarch	Rebel	Zealot	Empath	Seducer	Rogue
Hero	X			X				
Villain			X		X			
Sidekick						X		
Playmate							X	X
Mentor		X						

69

The use of metatypes can also help you to create and understand characters:

1. You can use metatypes directly in inventing a new character: 'My protagonist will be a scholar with a strong roguish streak, while his playmate/antagonist will be a senior hierarch.' Then you can add more detail: he's an inventive con-man who does his home work, she's a trusted manager at a casino. As you proceed with this fleshing-out, you might find that the germ of a plot begins to emerge.

2. You can also use metatypes to find the heart and soul of an existing character. If you realize that your heroine has elements of both scholar and seducer then you can use that insight in developing her further—and to populate the story with suitable playmates for the sexy brainbox.

You may be tempted to invent or seek out specifically erotic character types: Bad Boys, Bigshots, Ice Queens, Slave Girls... the list might be endless. Why go to the effort of working from archetypes and metatypes if you can just pick the desired item from a list of stock characters?

The problem is precisely that stock characters are too specific.

They are solutions looking for problems. Your work will be more real if you state the problem first and then develop a unique solution.

The Ice Queen that you develop around the spines of 'playmate', 'zealot' and 'hierarch' will be who she is for a reason. If you were to start with 'heroine', 'warrior' and 'seducer' you might end up with a very different Ice Queen. You won't necessarily expose your Ice Queen's internal makeup to the reader, but her metatypes (and your reasons for selecting them) will still be there and will affect how the character grows and is perceived.

The Ice Queen that you pluck from the stock character shelf has no such internal coherence. Lacking direction, she risks ending up as a stereotype.

The Flawed Character
Real people are never perfect, and neither should fictional characters be. Giving some appropriate flaws (whether mental or physical) to your characters adds depth and humanity.

A **minor flaw** has little effect on the story, but makes the character more believable and possibly more endearing. For example, a slight tendency to overspend would usually be a minor flaw, and would elicit sympathy from many readers.

A **major flaw** impacts the story directly. As with a minor flaw, a major flaw serves to deepen the character, but its main job is to drive the story. If the central conflict involves a man suffering from pathological shyness put in a position where he *must* get a date with an apparently unattainable woman, then his shyness is a major flaw; overcoming the flaw is central to the story's outcome.

Note: the fact that I chose overspending to illustrate a minor flaw, and shyness as an example of a major one, doesn't imply any judgement about the relative 'badness' of the flaws. The classification of 'major' or 'minor' is solely about the impact the flaw has on the character's story.

A **tragic flaw** ultimately causes the downfall of the flawed character. If you are writing upbeat erotica, you will not often create characters who are tragically flawed. In darker works, though, you might wish to do so. An example of a tragic flaw would be an erotic obsession that ends up driving the desired partner away forever.

Here is a (far from exhaustive) list of sample character flaws that might find a place in an erotic story:

- Addicted (to behavior or substances)
- Arrogant
- Bossy
- Closeted
- Dishonest
- Emotionally Remote
- False self-image
- Gossip
- Honest to a fault
- Impatient
- Insecure
- Jealous
- Lecherous
- Miserly
- Nosy
- Obsessive
- Phobic (any kind of irrational fear)
- Prejudiced
- Scatterbrained
- Selfish
- Shy
- Spendthrift
- Suspicious
- Timid
- Unfaithful
- Workaholic.

As you determine a character's flaws, also consider what might have caused them. Something in his career history? A childhood event? Some emotional burden he's been forced to bear through life? Or does the flaw come from the character's metatypes—a hierarch who's prone to arrogance, or a rogue who's too economical with the truth?

Even if the origins of a character's flaws never enter into the story, the fact that you know them allows you to portray the character more consistently, thus making her more real.

Fleshing Out

Once you've established some character spines and flaws, you can begin to flesh out the rest of the character. Much will flow from archetype and metatype, but certain aspects (such as physical traits) will not be influenced by these. Invent as you will. If you already have an outline for your story, then this will guide you too.

- **Background**—What is the character's social class? What was her family life like? What kind of education did she receive? Of what ethnicity and nationality is she? Is she religious? If so, how deeply and which religion?
- **Description**—What is the character's body type, hair color and eye color? Does she look striking or would she disappear in a crowd? What about her general posture, demeanor and attractiveness? What are her best and worst physical features—in her own eyes and in the eyes of others? Does she suffer from any physical problems?
- **Sexuality**—Is the character straight? Gay? Bi? How experienced is she, and how strong is her libido? What would she change about her sex life? Is she overtly sexual, or is she more demure? Is her sex life more about guilty secrets or innocent pleasures? Is she naturally dominant or submissive?
- **Mindset**—What morals/ethics does the character espouse? Is she a friendly person? Does she have a bitchy side? How open is she to new ideas? Is she more introverted or extroverted? Is it in her nature to be depressed, aggressive, passive, excited, jealous, cunning, aroused or lonely?

Remember that all these areas interact, both with the character's flaws and metatypes and with each other. A strict religious upbringing might affect the character's sexuality, or physical problems might be reflected in her mental outlook on the world.

Story Reveals Character

Up to now, we have discussed techniques that you can use to define characters at the planning stage. They can help you create and think about characters before you necessarily have a clear idea of what your plot will be.

Character can also emerge from plot. As soon as you begin your story, your characters start doing things. Then you can ask questions such as:

- **What does the character want, and why?**—Objectives and motives will inform the reader's judgement.
- **What choices does he make?**—Character emerges through actions, filtered by motive. Readers engage most when characters are forced into hard choices (for example, choosing the lesser of two evils), not when the choice is clear-cut.
- **How does it work out for him, and how does he respond?**—A character's reactions to setbacks and victories are telling.
- **How do other characters respond?**—A character can have a changing reputation within the story world. This in-story reputation informs the reader's perceptions. An undeserved reputation can generate sympathy, particularly if the character suffers because of others' erroneous impressions.
- **How does the character change?** Readers engage with protagonists who change or grow in some way. Major changes have a greater impact than minor ones.

Character Reveals Character

We will discuss one more technique that can help uncover character: asking the character herself. Some people recommend holding mock interviews with your characters, and that can work for certain writers.

If you find an interview too stilted, you could try something like the following. Imagine yourself sitting with your character in her home, and asking to see her photograph album. What kind of pictures are included? Which ones move the character most? Which has she torn out because they made her shudder with revulsion? Is there one she'd like to burn, if only she could bring herself to do it? Which picture makes her happiest? Which makes her squirm with embarrassment?

If she's not the sort of person to have a photo album, use some other collection of meaningful objects: the contents of her closet or nightstand, perhaps, or the jumble of shells, amber, flints and bone needles in the niche at the back of her hut.

Checklist of Character Essentials

1. Your protagonist must seem special in some way. You're free to write an erotic story about the girl-next-door, but she'd better move out from next-door (at least metaphorical) without delay.
2. Your protagonist should be flawed; too-perfect 'Mary Jane' characters don't ring true. Flaws can enrich a character. It's wise to keep your protagonist at least somewhat likeable though (unless you're specifically setting out to write a tale of alienation).
3. The reader should want your protagonist to achieve her erotic/romantic goals (and any other goals she may have).
4. The reader should care if the protagonist is in jeopardy.
5. The reader should also feel sympathy for the antagonist.
6. The protagonist should be transformed in some way by the events of the story.

Chapter Summary

- Character is at least as important in erotic fiction as it is in any other kind of fiction.
- Players drive the story through their actions; Voyeurs watch, report and judge.
- Archetypal characters fill specific story roles.
- Character metatypes provide spines around which characters can be fleshed out.
- You can capture an erotic character by means of BDSM (Background, Description, Sexuality, Mindset).
- Character is revealed through story.
- Character can also be revealed by the characters themselves.
- Major characters should be both extraordinary and flawed.
- Protagonists should undergo transformation.
- Effective characters engage the reader's sympathy.

2 Point-of-View

Having developed a set of interesting characters to populate your erotic story world, your task is then to show these characters going about their business. You must address two goals in doing this:

1. Explain the action (both in and out of the bedroom) precisely enough so that the reader can follow what is happening.

2. Draw the reader in to the lives and world of the characters, so that she roots for them, sympathizes with them, and worries about what might happen to them.

As we're about to see, these two requirements can pull a writer in opposite directions: clear explanations often create distance from the characters, while going closer to the characters can make it more difficult to provide clear explanations.

Why Not Just Write Everything Down?
The first requirement can be fully met by telling the reader of every event, action, thought, speech or background circumstance that affects the story. By giving such an exhaustive narrative, the storyteller seeks to expose[1] all the information needed for the reader to understand the story's twists and turns.

This approach is adopted by many writers who have learned their storytelling subconsciously, through exposure to the world of film. The movie-oriented storyteller aims his camera here and there, directing his audience's attention wherever required. He reveals things that are not witnessed by any character. He even flits into and out of various characters' minds, recording perceptions, thoughts and emotions at will.

---

1   This is why the process of delivering background information is called *exposition*.

The problem with this approach is that movies are not novels. Movies have to deal with limitations that don't apply on the page, while written fiction requires certain disciplines that are irrelevant to move makers. The difference boils down to this:

- A novel can transport the reader directly inside a character's head. No movie camera or cinema screen can manage this feat.

- A movie can show any physical event requred to tell the story, regardless of context. While a novelist can do this, it's generally best if she doesn't.

The following table contrasts the two storytelling styles.

Movie	Novel
Projected on the silver screen.	Projected inside the reader's head.
Reveals character through actions and dialogue.	Reveals character through actions, dialogue and the internal commentary of the character.
Portrays thought, emotion and passion indirectly through physical responses (or occasionally, waves crashing on rocks).	Portrays thought, emotion and passion either indirectly through physical responses, or directly by entering the character's mind. Free to exploit metaphors such as stormy seas if desired.
The story is generally told through the lens of a camera or the circuits of a special effects computer.	The story is generally told through the eyes and internal commentary of one or more characters.
Can masquerade as a novel (by having a voice-over 'read out loud') but this can pull the audience out of the action and detract from the overall experience.	Can masquerade as a movie (by means of a 'camera' that can go anywhere and record anything) but this can pull the reader away from the characters and detract from the overall experience.

The best movie makers work with the grain of their medium, not against it. They exploit the medium's strengths, such as its ability to communicate directly in audiovisual terms, to physically build dramatic scenes, to point the camera wherever required (even into virtual worlds that only exist inside special effects computers).

As a fiction writer, you need to play to your medium's strengths too. Telling a story through a series of freewheeling, movie-style cuts ends up being jarring to the reader (even if only subconsciously). Worse, every time you cut to some event that your character does not witness, or reveal some information she cannot know, you create distance between your characters and your readers.

By contrast, if you allow your characters to tell their tale through their experiences, perceptions and thoughts, then they will draw the reader into their world and their lives.

In an erotic story, there can be no doubt about which of these you want to achieve.

What is Point-of-View?

Point-of-view (POV) is the viewpoint from which a scene or story is written. It is one of the most powerful tools in the fiction writer's box of tricks for generating sympathetic, engaging characters, yet it's also one of the most misunderstood and misused—in mainstream fiction as well as in the erotic genre.

Fiction can be written in any of the following POVs:

POV	Examples
First-person	I went there, I did this
Second-person	You went there, you did this
Third-person	He went there, he did this

First Person

A first-person story is an eyewitness account, written from the viewpoint of the narrator. The story unfolds through the narrator's activities and experiences, along with her internal commentary and judgements.

Using a first-person narrator is one of the most powerful ways of expressing character and creating reader involvement. The story can be told in the narrator's unique voice, and be filled with her thoughts, insights and asides. Digressions and opinions seem natural, as long as they're in-character for the narrator. The first-person viewpoint generates instant sympathy—it's as close as a reader can get to walking a mile in the character's shoes (in fact it goes further than that: it lets the reader listen to the narrator's thoughts and look at the world through her eyes).

The main disadvantage of this viewpoint is that the narrator must be present in every scene—otherwise how could she report what happened? The more complex and multi-layered the story, the more difficult this becomes.

In erotic tales that include a wide variety of sex scenes and participants, the need to report everything through a single pair of eyes can be particularly problematic. The narrator's best friend might be going at it hammer and tongs in the next room, but (unless your narrator peeps through the keyhole) you'd be forced to omit the juicy details.

Of course, the friend might relate her bedroom experience after the scene was over. Similarly, the narrator (and thus the reader) could learn of events through letters, emails, or similar devices. Take care not to overdo this: the narrator should witness all key scenes. Why reduce a crucial dramatic moment to a piece of in-story gossip?

The Narrator and the Protagonist

A first-person story can be narrated by someone other than its protagonist. Perhaps the best-known example of this occurs in the Sherlock Holmes stories: Watson is the narrator while Holmes is the central character. Watson (and the reader) can still be mystified, long after Holmes has mentally solved the case. Also, the message

'Holmes is a genius' is easier to take if it comes from someone other than Holmes himself.

In an erotic story, such a separation can be awkward. The power of the first-person viewpoint comes from its ability to pull the reader into the narrator's life — including her sex life and emotional life. If the readers of Sherlock Holmes had been interested in what he got up to in the bedroom (and presuming that he and the good doctor were not lovers) then listening to Watson would have been no use whatsoever.

Where the narrator *is* the protagonist, the reader's perception of the character can be subtly shaded by the first-person voice. Consider the following two snippets:

1. *I won every time, of course. It was almost unfair to the others, being faced with so perfect a competitor.*

2. *She won every time, of course. It was almost unfair to the others, being faced with so perfect a competitor.*

The second example, by weakening the connection between the narratorial voice and the person being praised, seems less self-congratulatory and becomes easier to take.

Second Person

This form is not widely used, though it occasionally crops up in erotic works as well as in other genres. By its nature, writing in the second-person produces an artificial feel: *You woke up. The house was shuttered and empty. You went outside, wondering where everybody had gone…*

If you wish to cast the reader as a character in your story, this is the way to go. However, the reader is demonstrably *not* a character in your story, so the second-person viewpoint inevitably ends up feeling strained. If we accept the conceit that the reader is somehow participating in the story, why would it then be necessary to keep her appraised of what she's doing? She would surely know without being told.

Overall, this viewpoint is best avoided, or saved for specialized or experimental works where its drawbacks are acceptable.

Third Person

This is the most commonly used fictional viewpoint, but also the most complex and potentially problematic. Part of the complexity is that there are several variants of this POV. The most important distinction is between third-person omniscient and third-person limited.

The Third-Person Omniscient Narrator

The omniscient narrator does not figure as a character in the story. It is more like a disembodied voice, floating somewhere above the landscape and able to perceive and communicate whatever it will. It can slip inside any character's head to report on her thoughts and desires, and can inform the reader of any event, no matter how remote in time or space.

An omniscient narrator can write things like:

> Bob looked at the way Lisa's nipples peaked darkly under the sheer fabric of her blouse. Amused, Lisa gazed back at him with her grey eyes and he looked away guiltily, wondering if she'd noticed him ogling her—but it was all right, she'd seen him and she didn't mind. She was too busy concentrating on his tightly-muscled chest. Lisa wanted Bob as badly as he wanted her.

We've skipped from Bob's head to Lisa's, and back again, and forward, all in a single paragraph. In a phrase talking about Lisa, we described the color of her eyes, even though she'd hardly have been dwelling on that. There's no doubt about what the couple want, because the omniscient narrator can report exactly what they're thinking. But I hope you can see how the above passage jars every time it skips from one character to the other, and how we're never really pulled into either of their heads.

The omniscient voice can pull readers out of the story because it invites the question: 'Who is telling me all this stuff? Who could possibly know it, and why would they want to report it?' Even if a reader doesn't vocalize these concerns, they're still there, nagging at her subconscious and stopping her from engaging with the story and characters as deeply as she might.

The final disadvantage of this viewpoint is that it does not lend itself to mystery—there's a narrator right there telling the reader everything she needs to know, so what excuse can there be for withholding vital information?

Because of these problems, the omniscient narrator's strength— the ability to reveal anything, at any time—is less valuable than you might imagine in an erotic tale. If you decide to use this viewpoint, be sure that what you gain is worth the extra distance it creates between the reader and your characters.

The Third-Person Limited Narrator

This viewpoint closely follows a single character for a scene, a chapter, or sometimes even for an entire book. The term *'limited'* reflects the limitation placed on what you may tell the reader:

> *The third-person limited narrator may not inform the reader of anything that the viewpoint character does not know.*

This restriction is no different from the one faced by a first-person narrator. In the case of the first-person narrator, the logic is plain: *'If I wasn't there and didn't hear about it later, then I can't tell you about it.'*

This irrefutable logic doesn't apply with third-person stories: as we've just seen, the <u>omniscient</u> narrator can drop any piece of information at any time. Perhaps that's why so many writers find the <u>limited</u> version of this viewpoint to be difficult to grasp.

It's worth making the effort, because mastering this viewpoint is one of the most important steps you can take toward writing engaging characters. The power that this POV has to generate reader sympathy comes from various sources:

• You set aside some uninterrupted time (at least an entire scene) for the reader to spend in the company of the viewpoint character. No extraneous information or events are allowed to intrude.

• You only provide the reader with information that is available (and of interest) to the viewpoint character. The reader's experience mirrors the character's experience.

- In contrast with the first-person narrator, the outcome is more in doubt in a third-person tale. The first-person narrator at least ended up in a position where he had pen and paper, and the leisure and inclination to write. There are no such guarantees for a character in a third-person tale.

- The voice of the limited narrator fades into the background, to the point where the reader can ignore it. Compare with the omniscient narrator, who remains a clear and possibly distracting presence on the page.

Third-person limited stories, well-executed, can create the illusion that readers are sharing something important with the viewpoint characters. This leads to a sense of bonding. The fewer the distractions, the more intense this becomes.

A third-person limited story can follow one character from beginning to end, or it can switch to a different character at a suitable break-point, typically at the end of a chapter or scene. The ability to switch characters gives this viewpoint more flexibility than the first-person narrator could offer: if something important happens that your main character doesn't witness, just switch to a character who was there.

Switching viewpoints within a scene is not advisable; if you do that, then you're moving toward omniscience.

69

As with every writing choice you make, there are trade-offs to be considered. The principal trade-off with this viewpoint is that you have to work harder to introduce information that the character wouldn't see or care about.

Consider the problem of describing the viewpoint character. People don't usually go around mulling over the details of their physical appearance, so staying strictly in POV means you can't bombard the reader with descriptions of height, build, hair-color or whatever.

Some writers resort to the tried-and-trusted trick of providing the character with a mirror before which he can stand while checking off his features, one after another:

Two blue eyes stared back at him, chips of ice gazing from be-
low his unruly brown curls. He ran his fingers over the harsh
stubble that covered his chin, then over the cheekbones that had
been the breaking of so many hearts...

If you find yourself writing such piffle while trying to produce
a third-person limited piece, ask yourself what the character is *re-*
ally doing. Then remind yourself how silly it sounds:

'Phew, still got two blue eyes, check. They're looking kind of
icy today, but now I come to think of it they always did. Brown
hair, out of control as per normal. Check. Now what the hell is
this? More stubble? Isn't this damn beard ever going to stop
growing? Oh well, check. Boy, am I glad my cheekbones didn't
plump out during the night, women go mad for 'em...'

The mirror cliché is a cheap trick used by writers who can't be
bothered to deliver description in a more believable way (which
could be as simple as giving another character a good reason to
comment on the characteristic you wish to describe).

Even if you stoop to using this technique, it's only going to help
you once (you wouldn't be so cruel as to force *two* characters in
one story to make idiots of themselves in front of a mirror, would
you?)

69

Returning to the previous scenario between Lisa and Bob, and
adopting Bob as our limited viewpoint character, we might have
something like:

Bob looked at the way Lisa's nipples peaked darkly under the
sheer fabric of her blouse. Was it arousal that stiffened them, or
simply the chill evening air? He realized he was staring and
looked away guiltily, hoping his inspection hadn't been too obvi-
ous. If she'd noticed anything, she showed no sign. She simply
gazed at him with her clear grey eyes. He shifted uneasily, won-
dering what she'd think—and how she'd respond—if she knew
how much he desired her.

The detailed insights and easy description that the narrator provided in the first version have gone, but we've gained something better in return: closer character identification. We've moved from observing the character to *experiencing* the character.

Before we leave this topic, here's a question for you: why was it okay to mention the color of Lisa's eyes in the above sample? Answer below[1].

Level of Penetration

Beside the obvious kind of penetration you might find in erotic fiction, in third-person limited stories there's also the question of how deeply you inhabit your characters.

At the shallowest level, a third-person limited story could follow the viewpoint character without entering his mind at all. In this model, you portray characters much as a movie maker would. You show where they're looking without actually looking through their eyes:

> Bob glanced at his watch several times as he waited for Lisa to get changed. Finally she emerged from the bedroom.
> 'Do these shoes go with this dress?' she asked.
> Bob stared at the red patent stilettos, and then at Lisa's stocking-covered legs. He licked his lips, keeping his gaze well below her hemline. 'I guess,' he said.
> Lisa frowned. 'You didn't look at the dress at all.'

The above passage says nothing (directly) about what Bob is thinking or feeling. We know he's impatient, but only because he checked his watch. We know he's affected by Lisa's stockings and high heeled shoes, but only because of the way he studied them, licked his lips, and gave a vague answer to her question. The only clues to his state of mind are external ones.

Penetrating a little deeper, you might report on the character's thoughts and feelings, but from a distance:

---

1   The viewpoint character has the hots for Lisa, giving him the perfect reason to be interested in and to dwell on *any* of her physical attributes.

Bob grew more and more impatient, wondering how much longer Lisa would take getting changed. To his relief, she finally emerged from the bedroom.

'Do these shoes go with this dress?' she asked.

As far as Bob was concerned, the patent red stilettos looked great. The stockings looked great, too. After that, his interest in women's fashion kind of fizzled out. 'I guess,' he said.

Lisa frowned. 'You didn't look at the dress at all.'

Here, we relate Bob's thoughts to the reader, so we don't have to rely on physical cues to portray his feelings. But we're still not inhabiting his mind as deeply as we might:

Could his watch have stopped? No, the second hand was still crawling around the dial. Bob glanced at the bedroom door again. Why did women take so long to get ready? He had to stay calm. The last thing he wanted was to appear impatient.

'Do these shoes go with this dress?' Lisa asked when she finally emerged.

What a question; how was he supposed to know? Lisa's stockings and red patent stilettos were a different matter, though—different enough to make Bob sneak yet another look at her legs. 'I guess,' he said.

Lisa frowned. 'You didn't look at the dress at all.'

In this final passage, we're not describing Bob's thought processes from the outside; we're right there in his head, eavesdropping on his interior monologue. There's no need to add a tag such as *'he wondered'* to Bob's mental questions, because the viewpoint is embedded so deeply in his mind.

Note how the passage grew longer and more leisurely with each revision. Delving deeper brings out more details, takes more space, and naturally slows the pace of the storytelling.

There's no one correct level of penetration to use. You'll want to vary things from scene to scene, possibly even from paragraph to paragraph, choosing the most appropriate level. If you want to build intensity (during a moment of particular emotion or arousal, for example), then go deep. If you want to give the reader a break from that intensity, pull back.

The Unreliable Narrator

Each first-person narrator will have her own personality and agenda; she might be one hundred percent truthful or she might pepper her testimony with half-truths and outright lies.

Deep third-person narration can also be unreliable. The fact that the reader is eavesdropping on a character's thoughts doesn't mean those thoughts have to be true:

- The character might be lying to himself.
- He might be immersed in a private fantasy world.
- He might be a loser who's deeply invested in persuading himself that he's actually important and successful.

Any number of factors could create a dissonance between the character's perceptions and reality.

> 'See you Friday night, then?' I ask.
> Cathy glances at her friend. 'I'm going to be busy.'
> I can tell she wants to say 'Yes,' but she's embarrassed because her friend is there. One day I'll get her away from him and then it'll be different.
> It's lucky for Cathy I'm so patient; plenty of guys would have moved on after six months, soul-mates or no.
> Not me, though.

If you use unreliable narrators, give your reader enough clues to evaluate their information—and the more important the lie, the clearer the clue should be.

Switching Viewpoints

As we've seen, third-person limited viewpoint builds unrivaled reader sympathy. Following one character for an entire novel is the ultimate way to make the reader care—but strength in one area inevitably leads to trade-offs in others:

- By definition, that closeness can only apply to one character.
- Just as with the first person narrator, the single viewpoint character must witness (or at least learn of) all key events.

A more flexible and even-handed approach is to switch view-point characters at suitable points (usually the end of a chapter or scene). The advantages of this are:

- Reader sympathy extends to more characters (if less deeply).

- Careful choice of POV character brings more impact to each scene. Generally, give viewpoint to the character who has the most at stake in the scene.

- Exposition may be easier. If a secondary character knows or does something significant, switching to that character lets you show the event to the reader.

- It can help build tension. You can insert a mini-cliffhanger each time you switch to a different viewpoint.

- It can help control pace. Manageable, varied chunks of narrative can read 'faster' than monolithic blocks.

- You can cut rapidly back and forward between two points of view, showing different perceptions of the same events. If used sparingly, this can be an exceptionally powerful way to develop erotic scenes, by spending a page or so in each character's head in turn. There is no better way to bring out the empathy and mutual insecurity that makes your characters human as well as sexual.

- A skilled author can deepen characterization by using a distinct and appropriate voice to report the thoughts and experiences of each viewpoint character.

When you switch POV, establish the new viewpoint character quickly. If you use one viewpoint per chapter, you might include the character's name in the chapter title. Alternatively, you can simply use the character's name within the first line or two of the new scene. The important thing is not to leave the reader groping, or even unaware that viewpoint has just switched—it will be jarring later, if she suddenly realizes that she's reading about Bob and not Lisa after all.

Mixing Viewpoints

Occasionally, you might need more flexibility than a single viewpoint can offer. Third-person viewpoints are seldom a problem in this regard: in the omniscient view you can follow any character you like, while in the limited view you can access as many viewpoints as desired as long as you deal with the transitions properly.

What about mixing first-person narrative with other viewpoints, or having a first-person story told by multiple narrators? That's more complex, and can lead to issues of believability for the reader. Here are some alternatives that other writers have tried, with varying degrees of success:

- Having first-person chapters intermixed with third-person chapters. This can work once the reader gets used to it, but it begs the question: 'Who wrote the third-person parts?' It's scarcely credible that the narrator would research what everybody else was doing and then intermix third-person passages into her own first-person account, so the arrangement is a constant reminder that the novel is a work of artifice. It can work, but the writing and story had both better be outstanding—powerful enough to compensate for the distracting nature of the presentation.

- Having a first-person story where the narrator is talking to somebody who launches into his own, different first-person narrative, leading to a 'story within a story'.

- Similarly, you could have a third-person story where one of the characters tells a first-person story—another version of the 'story within a story' idea.

- Having a different first-person story unfolding in each chapter. To help keep things clear, assign headings that explain who will be talking in the coming chapter.

Until you are comfortable working with your chosen viewpoint on its own, it is probably best to avoid the more exotic hybrids.

Strengths and Weaknesses

Your choice of point-of-view will depend on what you wish to achieve in your story. Each POV has an area where it excels, and each has its drawbacks and difficulties:

	First Person	Third-person Omniscient	Third-person Limited
Ease of Exposition	Easy where the information concerns the narrator, otherwise requires more work.	Easy: any information can be given to the reader at any time.	Easy where the information concerns the POV character, otherwise requires more work.
Character Sympathy	Strong: 'I will tell you my story in my own words.'	Weak: 'Let me tell you about this guy.'	Strong: 'Come with this character and share her journey.'
Potential for Mystery	Strong: anything unknown to the narrator can be made mysterious.	Weak: why is the author withholding crucial information?	Strong: anything unknown to the viewpoint character can be made mysterious.
Narratorial Flexibility	Constrained: must stay with narrator (tricks can be used to get around this).	Unconstrained: the tale can focus on anybody and anything desired.	Supple: can switch viewpoint characters at scene or chapter breaks.
Erotic Engagement	Strong: 'I will explain exactly what I did and how it felt.'	Weak: 'Let me tell you a story about this guy who had great sex.'	Strong: 'Share this character's journey and come with her.'

Chapter Summary

- Novels are not movies. Don't simply try to recreate a movie-style story on paper.

- **First-person viewpoint:** the story is told in the first-person by a narrator who is present in the story. Exposition is limited to what the narrator experiences or perceives.

- **Second-person viewpoint:** the story is told in the second-person. This viewpoint is seldom used but may be of interest for specialized or experimental works.

- **Third-person Omniscient:** the story is told in the third-person by a narrator who is not present in the story but who knows everything about the story world. No limitations are placed on the information the reader can receive.

- **Third-person Limited:** the story is told in the third-person by a narrator who fades to near-invisibility, with the limitation that the reader may only be told what the viewpoint character experiences or perceives.

- In third-person limited narratives, the level of penetration can vary from a distant view where only the character's actions are reported, to a close view where the reader is brought deeply into the character's mind.

- Each viewpoint has strengths and weaknesses that (together with your instincts and your intention for the piece) should inform your choice of viewpoint.

3 Plot and Structure

What is Plot?

Plot is the sequence of causes and effects that ripples through a story. You can think of a plot as a chain[1] of events as illustrated below. The chain is anchored at the leftmost extremity by the beginning of the story, and at the rightmost extremity by its end. Every link within the chain corresponds to a plot event, and connects to its neighbors, in the sense that every plot event within the story is caused by a previous event and causes a subsequent one.

Beginning   End

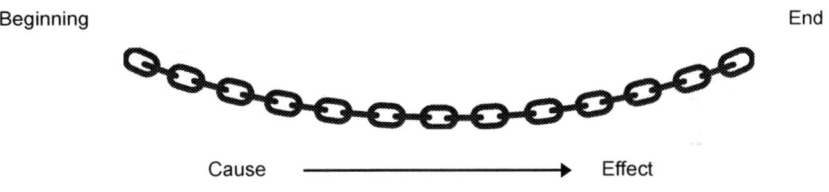

Cause   ——————————▶   Effect

Fig 3-1. Plot as a chain of events.

A story's plot-chain is sometimes called the *through-line*, indicating that it comprises the irreducible pathway through the story. When you summarize a story or a movie, you're probably talking about its through-line.

A novel-length work usually has a number of sub-plots weaving in and out of the main through-line. A sub-plot forms its own mini-storyline, possibly including its own characters, and adds complexity and interest to the story as a whole. Obviously, a sub-plot also has a through-line, and can be considered as a chain of lesser events hanging from the main plot-chain.

---

1   Ironically, BDSM stories in particular have a reputation for often lacking a solid plot. You'd think the writers would be familiar with chains.

With sub-plots in the picture, a more complex (but still highly simplified) 'plot-shape' begins to emerge:

Beginning   End

Fig 3-2. A sub-plot branching
from and rejoining
the through-line.

Not every sub-plot branches and reconnects so neatly. Sub-plots often connect several times, or are closely entwined around the main plot-chain. They can have their own independent beginnings or ends, and even their own sub-plots.

Sometimes, a sub-plot is inadvertently left hanging and unresolved, in which case it is called a 'loose end'. Visualizing your story in terms of the chains of cause and effect that make up its various through-lines can give you a better handle on managing complexity and on avoiding loose ends.

What about two completely unconnected through-lines? For example:

Beginning   End

Fig 3-3. Parallel, unconnected
through-lines
(not recommended)

While it is possible for a story to contain two parallel through-lines as shown in Figure 3-3, it doesn't make sense. The unrelated plot lines might make the work seem 'busier' but they cannot make it richer or more satisfying. Why not just write two separate stories? It is interaction, rather than disconnection, that generates interest. Multiple plot strands come into their own when they are interwoven; when they join, split, reconnect, and dance around one another; and when the consequences of their collisions resonate through the rest of the story.

Here are some additional simplified plot shapes that are potentially more interesting:

Beginning   End

Fig 3-4. Sub-plot with independent beginning, merging into main story.

Beginning   End

Fig 3-5. Sub-plot with independent end, branching off from main story.

Beginning   End

Fig 3-6. Mostly independent sub-plot impacting main story at one point.

In real stories, the interactions between various through-lines will be more complex. Multiple strands may split off at various points, usually to merge back again as the story approaches its conclusion. Regardless of complexity, the individual strands will still be there. Train yourself to be aware of them. Tease out the strands in stories you read and movies you watch: it will help you keep track of your own work.

Seek out opportunities for your sub-plots to impact one another, or your main plot. Sub-plots are not self-contained mini-stories that happen to join up occasionally. No matter how enthralling or erotic the events in one story area might be, it is the intersection of different through-lines that brings your story to life[1].

Of course, you could write a novel-length work with no sub-plots, just as you could write a story with no secondary characters and thus no dialogue or other contact. However, such a story would lack the richness that a more multi-layered approach could bring. It is easier to tell a compelling tale when you have enough elements (of whatever type) to set up interesting interactions between them.

On the other hand, if you are setting out to write a novella or a short story, the importance of sub-plots fades or disappears altogether. The shorter the work, the less able it is to support a sub-plot—but also the less need it has for complexity.

Whether you have one plot chain or many, each must be strong enough to persuade the reader that it is real. Leaving a single loose end by failing to bring a chain of events to a satisfactory conclusion will disappoint the reader (if the events were important enough to mention, surely they're important enough to wrap up?)

Take equal care to avoid 'loose beginnings', which are events that occur with no reason (or at least, no reason that the reader can discern). That is not to say that the story must start at the beginning of the main through-line, with all sub-plots branching off as effects of an earlier cause. As shown in the example plot shapes, it's quite possible to have multiple story threads running indepen-

1   The TV series *Friends* is not known for eroticism, but one episode features Ross's sexual fantasy about *Star Wars* character Princess Leia. We also see Chandler confiding to Ross that against his will, he imagines his mother during sex. These two sub-plots collide in the final scene, with Ross gazing at the object of his desire, Rachel, in her *Star Wars* costume—only to be distracted by Chandler's confession into imagining his own mother in the outfit, with a consequent loss of libido. Here, the power of the ending comes from the collision of the two sub-plots that the episode has developed.

dently, each with its own start. However, you should avoid having events occurring *within* the action of the story that cannot be traced back to any cause.

A prime example of this is the *Deus ex Machina*[2] occurrence. If your plot includes such an occurrence—or any event that 'just happens', ask yourself why you introduced the event. Was it to solve some story problem? Discerning readers will not be satisfied by such a solution. They expect to be able to recognize where every plot development came from, and may become tetchy if things simply appear out of left-field. At the very least, pave the way for an unanticipated event by foreshadowing[3] it, so that the reader can see with hindsight that the event made sense.

By all means surprise your readers, but do so in a way that leaves them thinking, *Wow, I should have seen that coming!* rather than simply, *What the…?*

What are the Essential Elements of Plot?

When thinking about story construction, it's helpful to understand the elements that make up almost every plot. By this I don't mean story-specific events and scenes; I mean the higher-level conceptual elements that you will develop and manipulate as you create your story. These higher level elements can be enumerated by means of an acronym, COBRA:

- Character
- Objective
- Barrier
- Resolution
- Aftermath.

---

2   *Deus ex Machina:* 'God from the Machine'. Ancient Greek dramatic conflict was sometimes resolved by the Gods being lowered onto the stage by means of a winch-like machine. The playwright, rather than the plot, required this intervention. It presumably worked for the ancient Greeks, for whom the Gods would have been a tangible interventionist presence. Modern audiences are unlikely to be so credulous.

3   Foreshadowing is the dropping of a subtle hint that justifies later plot developments. The reader might miss the hint at the time but later she says, *'Aha!'*. Compare with the red herring, which is a hint dropped with the intention to mislead (used more in mystery than in erotic fiction, perhaps, but such misdirection can still be useful in certain erotic stories).

The above ordering reflects the sequence in which the story elements are typically developed.

Character – the protagonist, or main story actor. Since the story revolves around the protagonist, it is usually best to introduce this character early. It would make little sense, for example, to devote time to explaining objectives and barriers while leaving the reader in the dark as to whom these objectives and barriers apply.

In an erotic story, the protagonist will inevitably be (or will become) a sexual being, and sexuality of some kind will normally play an important part in her desires and actions. However, jumping into a sex scene on the first page can be off-putting to readers; a slow build up to overt eroticism is often preferable. Consider putting your protagonist in an interesting (perhaps titillating) opening situation where her sensuality—and the nature of the story to come— can be made clear without necessarily forcing her into an immediate sexual act.

Objective – the protagonist's goal. This may be directly erotic in nature (win the desired lover, escape the rapacious slave owner, persuade the reluctant spouse). Alternatively, the objective can be more prosaic, but in this case it should open the way for sexual scenes.

The commonplace objective of winning a promotion, for example, may spill into sexuality if the character's nymphomaniacal boss insists that one favor should be traded for another: the objective is not directly sexual but can still lead to sexually-oriented action.

Barrier – the obstacle to the goal. Often, but not always, the barrier takes the form of a living opponent: perhaps a love-rival, or a rapacious Master or Mistress, or simply a reluctant lover (the opponent does not have to be a villain).

Why must there be a barrier? Because keeping the protagonist from achieving her goal creates conflict. It forces her to be active, to show her character, to do interesting things that engender reader sympathy. Conflict propels your story—and keeps your reader turning the pages.

Resolution – the turning point of the conflict that decides whether the character achieves the desired objective. If you want to tell a happy and upbeat tale, then provide a resolution that's in the character's favor (or make the character realize that her true desire was something else all along, in which case the true objective was 'hidden' from the character—though not necessarily from the reader). The romantic genre provides a classic example of this in the hate-relationship that turns into love.

Erotic novels often have upbeat endings, though this is not always so. For example, *Story of O*, Pauline Réage's classic erotic novel, has two endings, neither of which are upbeat and one of which is extremely dark.

Aftermath – some erotic stories will find a satisfactory ending at the point of resolution, but because eroticism always involves feelings, you can often achieve a better closure if you give your characters a few pages (or at least a few moments) to absorb the new state of affairs emotionally, showing how they have come to terms (or not) with the outcome.

69

You might have noticed that I wrote, 'the elements that make up almost every plot' above. It is possible to write erotic novels that lack one or more of the above elements. Returning to the *Story of O*, we have a main **character**, O, who has an **objective**, which is to please her lover, René, and thus to win his love and attention.

O faces a **barrier**—pleasing René means that she must submit herself to a deepening spiral of sexual enslavement and mistreatment by his friends and associates. The book closes with a brief **aftermath** in which O accepts her fate.

What is lacking is **resolution**. The story has no climactic struggle where O achieves, or fails to achieve, her objective. She simply submits, and submits, and submits. Her sole transformation is to become more submissive to more people—a tendency that was clear from the first page, and that holds no surprises and no hint of conflict.

Perhaps for this reason, many readers have found that *Story of O* became tedious once the initial BDSM stage-setting has been done—and indeed Réage is reported to have said that the first sixty pages almost wrote themselves, with the remainder being driven by her desire to finish the novel.

None of this is to deny *Story of O's* status as a cult novel, or as a masterpiece of erotic literature. The book was ground-breaking when first published in the 1950s; over the intervening decades it has rocked worlds, including mine. Nevertheless, many modern readers find themselves unsatisfied with the introspective turn the work takes after its electrifying opening, and wishing it delivered more of the *Story* promised by the title.

I will briefly compare *Story of O* with a contemporary erotic novel (one that's less literary and more commercial) in Appendix A, *Erotica, Literature and Commercialism.*

Plot, Subject and Theme

Literary works carry a deeper message than the simple sequence of cause-and-effect that makes up the plot. This message is the 'theme' of the work: some larger question or issue that the reader can take away and consider. Not every writer consciously develops a theme, but that doesn't prevent theme from emerging. If you have created a rich, coherent, interesting story, the chances are that readers will find a theme there, even if you never intended one.

Theme is not the same as plot. It would also be a mistake to confuse a story's subject with its theme.

Imagine a tale about the erotic relationships between a heroine and two men, both of whom compete for her. One suitor—we'll say he's the CEO of a large corporation—is a sophisticate with a million-dollar lifestyle that includes yachts, private jets, and apartments in several world cities. To put more of an erotic spin on things, let's say this CEO doesn't leave the power games in the boardroom—he brings them into the bedroom too.

Sometimes the heroine enjoys these games, but sometimes she finds them overwhelming. That's when she turns to lover number two, a lowly artist who can't compete when it comes to living the high life, but whose creativity, gentle temperament and Bohemian lifestyle still appeal to her.

From this sketch, we have the beginnings of character (the hero-

ine and her suitors), an objective (to achieve a satisfactory relationship outcome, which might be as simple as making a choice or as
complex as seducing both lovers into a *ménage à trois*), and a barrier
(neither man can give the heroine everything she wants, and neither is likely to give way or to tolerate being cuckolded).

The plot is the cause-and-effect sequence that determines who
(if anybody) will end up with whom. The subject of the story is
the three-way relationship between the heroine and the two men.
The theme will emerge from the writer's development of the story:
it could be *'money can't buy love'* or *'bigamy is underrated'* or even
'poverty sucks'.

Three-Act Structure

Humans have a natural tendency to think and to communicate
in sequences of three:

- Birth, Life, Death
- Wooing, Marriage, Happy Ever After (or not)
- Wood, Straw, Brick (not to mention Huff, Puff, Blow)
- Blood, Sweat, Tears
- Sex, Drugs, Rock'n'Roll
- Life, Liberty, the Pursuit of Happiness
- Three strikes and you're out.

Trios of related ideas pervade our world and our thinking (not
to mention the utterances of our would-be-leaders—have no doubt
that political speech writers understand which patterns resonate in
the electors' brains).

It's not surprising, then, that humans have a natural tendency
to tell, and to respond to, stories that take place in three Acts.

Act One: Seduction and Foreplay

What crucial job must the opening of a story accomplish? Some
authorities will answer, *'To introduce the protagonist'*, or *'To set the
scene'*, or *'To state the problem that drives the story'*.

Those are all valid things to do at the beginning of any story.
Some of them might even be crucial. But there is one task that, if
not handled properly, renders the rest of the story irrelevant:

The most important task accomplished in the First Act is
to seduce the reader into continuing into the Second Act.

All those answers about stating the story problem and so on are
merely parts from the kit of tools that you will use to accomplish
this goal.

The point is that it's not enough to learn a checklist of what must
be done by the end of Act One[1]. When introducing the protagonist,
you must also use your knowledge of character to make that protagonist compelling, otherwise why should the reader care? When
you show an objective and a barrier, you must work to make the
conflict palpable for the reader, otherwise why should she be concerned about whether the barrier can be overcome?

Checklists have their uses, but please don't consider them in
isolation. Back them up with every piece of knowledge you ever
gain about the craft of writing—and also with your own talent and
creative imagination.

Having said that, here are some tasks to be addressed by the
first Act of a three-Act story:

- Introducing your protagonist. If you have a story outline in
  mind but are not sure of who the protagonist is, ask yourself: *'Who has most at stake?'*; *'Who undergoes the most significant
  change?'*; *'Whose story is this?'*
- Identifying the objective desired by the protagonist and the barrier that must be overcome to achieve that objective.
- Establishing the world or setting in which the story takes place
  (modern corporate office; fantasy castle; regency mansion; vam-
  pire-haunted mountains; futuristic space station...)
- Establishing the overall tone of the story (erotic romance; hard-
  core BDSM; glamorous espionage; out-and-out fantasy; sophisticated satire; bawdy comedy...)

Act One should be long enough to perform the above scene-
setting tasks. However, it is not where your story will happen and
eventually it will be time to propel the protagonist (and hopefully
the reader) into Act Two.

The trip from Act One to Act Two is made on a one-way ticket.

1   This does not, of course, prevent me from offering such a list.

Even if your story location remains the same, your protagonist should find herself facing a different and more challenging set of circumstances, with no way back to the comfort zone of Act One. In *Story of O*, for example, the opening shows O and her lover together in a taxi. He begins to ritualistically undress her. At this point, O could refuse the challenge being set for her. She could tell the driver to stop, leave the taxi and continue with her life, but she chooses not to do any of these things. Instead, she obeys her lover and is delivered to Roissy, the establishment where she is to be trained and enslaved.

Once O has passed through the doorway into Roissy there can be no going back: she has made the transition to Act Two. Even if she were the kind of character who might try to escape, or who would refuse to obey her new Masters, there could be no return to her previous innocent condition.

Like O, your protagonist should pass through a one-way door to Act Two. He might go eagerly or he might have to be dragged, kicking and screaming, away from the comforting world of Act One (in fact, resistance can add depth by revealing character details or flaws). The important point is that your protagonist must wind up being propelled into Act Two, with no way of backing out of whatever he's gotten himself into.

Act Two: The Main Event

Act Two is where the story happens. You spent Act One establishing Character, Objective and Barrier; now is the time to develop those elements as you send your protagonist in pursuit of his objective and watch him struggling to overcome the barrier.

Your protagonist will doubtless engage in several sex scenes during this Act, leading to the question, *'How much sex is appropriate?'* If you're writing erotica in the hope of selling your work to a specific market, then the best way to answer this question is to consult the publisher's guidelines, or to inspect a few of their books. You might well receive an answer along the lines of *'Sexual activity should comprise half of the overall novel,'* or *'Every chapter must have a major scene.'*

But what if you're not writing to a set of commercial requirements, but crafting a story that *you* want to tell (and hopefully sell)? How much sex is appropriate then?

The answer is clear: as much as your story needs.

In making this decision, consider what drives the eroticism in your story. If you're using sex to spice up a mainstream story (in other words, one that's not erotic by nature) then you will need many sex scenes; many mainstream novels often include generous helpings of sex nowadays, and you're going to want to up the ante on those. You might find that your story suffers because you're not able to devote enough resources to its development (remember that every page spent on describing an erotic encounter is a page that is not available to develop the through-line of the story).

Another class of erotic stories have sex built in from the foundations up. These are not stories where characters pursuing everyday goals happen to have lots of sex; they are stories *about* sex. Conflict, drama and character can all be erotic and/or romantic in nature. If you incorporate sexuality into the very bones of your tale, the answer to the question *'How much sex should there be?'* will come naturally—and even on pages with no sexual activity whatsoever, erotic heat will still seep from the story's architecture.

Chapter 4, *The Erotic Promise,* discusses this idea of 'spiced up mainstream' versus 'fundamentally erotic' stories in more depth.

As well as bringing out erotic themes, Act Two must also develop the other aspects of your story. The reader wants to get to know the protagonist better, so show your characters doing interesting and challenging things. Act Two is also your opportunity to develop the objective and the barrier. Perhaps the protagonist experiences some change that forces her to expand or re-evaluate her objective. Perhaps the forces ranged against her throw some new variables into the mix. Perhaps she overcomes the initial barrier only to be confronted with a more challenging one.

In Act Two, you are looking to create a sense of 'rising action', where the tension ratchets up and the stakes get ever higher. The protagonist's objective seems further and further out of reach, and the barrier more intractable—no matter how hard the character works. In short: be mean to your protagonist.

If you find yourself falling in love with your hero or heroine, steel yourself and hurt what you love. Readers want to watch characters struggling against the odds and triumphing (if at all) because of their cleverness, strength, sexiness, fortitude, etc. Make things too easy and your audience will lose interest.

By the end of Act Two, if you've done a good job of tension building, your protagonist's outlook will appear bleak. She might even appear doomed to fail. Romance writers call this the 'black moment', when things can't possibly get any worse. Erotica writers would do well to take a leaf out of the Romance writer's book, and incorporate 'black moments' in their own work.

Once you reach the crisis point, it's time to send the protagonist through another one-way door, into Act Three.

Act Three: Climax and Afterglow

The first two Acts dealt with the Character, Objective and Barrier. Act Three must present the Resolution and Aftermath.

By the time the reader reaches Act Three, she will (if you have done your job properly) be itching to see whether the protagonist achieves his objective, and how he overcomes the seemingly insurmountable barrier that has developed by the end of Act Two.

This happens most powerfully when the protagonist faces an impossible situation, yet you provide a credible solution that the reader didn't see coming.

Readers might forgive an ending that was somewhat predictable, but you should make every effort to provide them with a surprise. They will not accept a *Deus-ex-Machina* ending, or one that is not (within the world of the story, at least) believable.

The ending should also tie up any loose ends. Now is the time to think about the through-lines of every sub-plot you used, and to make sure none have been forgotten.

Finally, many readers look for a sense of meaning or closure at the end of a story, particularly one where they've invested deeply in the characters and the fictional world. An over-abrupt ending can leave them feeling vaguely cheated—satisfied with the resolution, but nevertheless with the sense that there should have been something more.

If you were directing a movie, you probably wouldn't cut to the credits right after the climactic scene. Instead, you might follow the characters for a little longer, to give a sense of where they're headed. You might pull the camera back to show something of the world in which they now exist, or let it linger on some object of significance. Techniques that work in movies don't necessarily translate to the written page, but it's worth considering ways of doing something similar, perhaps by showing your characters coming to terms with their new state. Or, if the story opened with a figurative question, then the ending can close the circle by demonstrating that the question has been answered.

Upbeat versus Downbeat Endings

The discussion so far has focused on erotic stories that end on an upbeat note. If yours does not (if you're exploring the darker side of human nature, for example, or writing a tale of erotic horror) then you should give extra consideration to the buildup and release of tension in the second and third Acts.

For example, you might write a more upbeat second Act, rather than descending all the way to a black moment (since you're going to have an even blacker moment at the story's climax).

Fiction thrives on unpredictability and readers thrive on surprises (though not on random surprises: every unexpected turn of events should make sense with hindsight).

A tale where the protagonist's fortunes simply go from bad to worse offers no *Aha!* moment for the reader to relish—but if you're setting out to explore a character's fall to the uttermost depths, this pattern of decline may be exactly what you want. In that case you can still lighten the journey with a few upbeat moments. A glimmer of hope, cruelly snatched away, can add to the tension and make the story all the more powerful—and more engaging than a relentless descent into despair.

Figures 3-7 to 3-9 opposite show how the outlook for the protagonist might vary during the course of an upbeat story and two downbeat stories. Figure 3.7 (upbeat) shows a conflict-laden, steadily worsening second Act followed by a turning point and a victory for the protagonist. Figure 3.8 (downbeat) offers the protagonist (and the reader) several glimmers of hope during the second Act before the *coup de grâce*, while Figure 3-9 (also downbeat) shows the relentlessness of a story with no such relief.

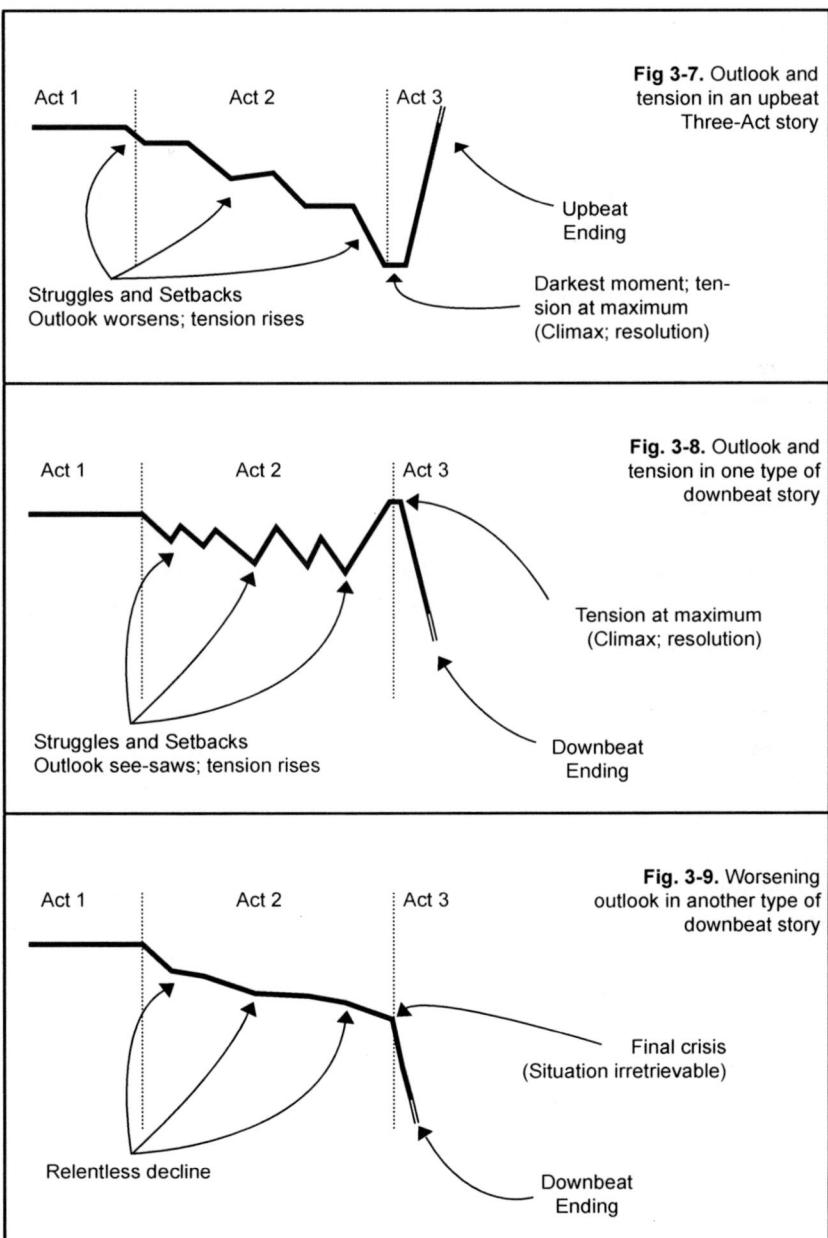

Fig 3-7. Outlook and tension in an upbeat Three-Act story

Act 1   Act 2   Act 3

Upbeat Ending

Struggles and Setbacks
Outlook worsens; tension rises

Darkest moment; tension at maximum
(Climax; resolution)

Fig. 3-8. Outlook and tension in one type of downbeat story

Act 1   Act 2   Act 3

Tension at maximum
(Climax; resolution)

Struggles and Setbacks
Outlook see-saws; tension rises

Downbeat Ending

Fig. 3-9. Worsening outlook in another type of downbeat story

Act 1   Act 2   Act 3

Final crisis
(Situation irretrievable)

Relentless decline

Downbeat Ending

The Hero's Journey

The term 'Hero's Journey' (already mentioned in Chapter 1) refers to an archetypal story-shape encountered everywhere from the ancient myths of our ancestors right up into the science fiction age with movies such as *Star Wars* and *The Matrix*. In between, it also showed up in a swathe of classical storytelling including Beowulf, Wagner, Tolkien and the *Wizard of Oz*. It is so deeply ingrained into our cultural consciousness that its ideas resonate even when we don't recognize them.

In essence, the Hero's Journey involves a character being challenged to leave his familiar world, entering a world of adventure, learning lessons, winning allies, contending with enemies, winning a prize and returning to his own world.

An in-depth examination of the Hero's Journey is beyond the scope of this book, and its focus on the structures of mythic adventure does not always apply to erotic stories. On the other hand, narrative elements and patterns from the Journey pervade so much of our storytelling that writers can end up using them quite unconsciously, without ever having heard of the term.

So even if you don't wish to set out to use any particular 'template' for your stories, it's worth gaining a basic knowledge of this story-pattern—and as you understand it better, and ponder on the chord it strikes with audiences, you might just decide to take parts of it for your own use.

Turn to Appendix B, *The Hero's Journey (with pop-culture context)* if you wish to learn more. As well as presenting a summary of the stages and character archetypes encountered in the Hero's Journey, it includes notes on adapting the Journey to erotic storytelling, and references to source material.

69

For the immediate purpose of erotic and romantic storytelling, I will present a slimmed-down version that you may find to be lighter on its feet, more flexible, and generally easier to get along with than the Journey's fully developed masculine form:–

The Heroine's Journey

Act One

1. The heroine is shown in her comfort zone (at home in her everyday world). She may have experienced some injury or have some character flaw that hinders her from fulfilling her potential. The flaw may prevent her from leaving the comfort zone; conversely, the comfort zone may enable her to tolerate the flaw.
2. Some life-changing event (disturbance) impels the heroine out of her comfort zone and toward erotic adventure.
3. The heroine may be reluctant to leave her comfort zone (often because of her old injury, or the associated character flaw).
4. The heroine decides or is compelled to leave her comfort zone. She crosses the threshold into the sensual world of Act Two.

Act Two

1. A friend, mentor, or other allies may be present. They guide the heroine and help her overcome the effects of her injury or flaw.
2. There are several encounters and confrontations as the erotic action escalates along with the stakes. The opponent does not have to be a villain, just someone standing between the heroine and her objective. He might even be the target of the heroine's sexual interest, in which case his opposition might be no more than indifference.
3. The heroine experiences a black moment. Her opponent may have a hand in this, but her injury or character flaw might also play a part in bringing her low.

Act Three

1. The heroine overcomes her character flaw and achieves her goals, possibly aided by some (self) knowledge or totem that she gained during Act Two.
2. The heroine receives her ultimate erotic reward and returns home (metaphorically if not physically).

Creating Plot

- Imagine a situation...

- What could go wrong with it?

- What could have caused it? What might the consequences be? (Remember, plot is cause and effect. If you invent plausible and interesting sequences of cause and effect, you are inventing plot).

- Play *'What If...?'* What if X happened? Then what if Y happened? What if that led to Z? Chances are that the first few answers to pop into your head will be obvious ones. Don't settle for that: dream up a dozen answers and choose the best, the most intriguing, the most startling. Then dream up a dozen more. Don't listen to the internal censor that insists your ideas are no good: record everything. Reserve judgement for later and let your imagination roam free.

- Set up expectations that seem reasonable for your characters (and thus the reader) and then twist things to deliver a setback. The result that seemed so achievable turns out, with hindsight, to have been hopelessly optimistic. The reversal, though unimaginable at the time, proves to be logical, even inevitable. The real outcome was hidden until it occurred, meaning that the *plot twists* in an unexpected direction. The more justified the original expectations and the more credible the reversal, the more believable your story will be and the more tension you will create.

- Do the same thing with negative expectations, in order to turn a hopeless situation around.

- After each scene, allow the affected characters to reflect on what happened. Give them time to come to terms with any setbacks and to decide what to do next. This period of reflection is just as applicable to a sex scene as it is to any other kind of scene. By balancing each action scene with a reflective aftermath, you bring out character, control pace, and prevent your story from degenerating into a headlong rush toward the ending.

- Think of an ending and then identify some of the stories that might lead up to it. What kind of beginning would resonate with the ending you have in mind?
- Think of a title and then invent the story that goes with it.
- Invent a character and then ask questions about him, his goals, motivation, background and relationships. Range as widely as you will, but make sure that at least some of those questions begin with, *'What If…?'*
- 'Rip and Mix' from existing genres and stories. I'm not suggesting you steal plots or characters wholesale, but every writer is influenced by what has been before. Think *Sexy Science Fiction* or *Perverted Pride and Prejudice.* Fairytales and folklore provide a rich seam that's been mined by several successful erotic authors, but there's still room for original takes—and there's no need to limit yourself to any particular genre. If a story has the potential for erotic conflict, it has the potential to become erotica.

Chapter Summary

- *Plot* is the ripple of cause-and-effect that drives a story.
- The *through-line* is the key pathway through a story.
- In longer works, interacting *sub-plots* add richness and complexity.
- Identifying *through-lines* helps manage story complexity and avoids *loose ends* and *loose beginnings.*
- The essential elements of plot are *Character, Objective, Barrier, Resolution* and *Aftermath.*
- The *Three-Act Structure* is both primal and useful as a way of organizing your story.
- In the *Three Act Structure*, transitions from one act to the next are one-way trips.
- Using elements from the *Hero's Journey* can add resonance to your tale, even if you simplify them.
- Of all the plot-generating questions you might ask, *'What If…?'* is the most powerful.

4   The Erotic Promise

The Erotic Promise

Like any other piece of fiction, the erotic story makes promises to its reader. The reader begins the story in hope; as she turns the opening pages and decides to continue, this hope crystalizes into an expectation of what the story will deliver by its end.

The first promise of an erotic story is to arouse the reader.

Given the wide range of literary tastes and sexual preferences, no single erotic tale can be a turn-on for everybody, but unless your work strikes a spark of sexual response with at least some readers, it will be a failure. As an erotica author, you *must* fulfil the first promise.

The second promise is to entertain.

Written erotica can be as entertaining as any other storytelling mode. Beside turning the reader on, an erotic story might also amuse, amaze, mystify, scare or thrill her—or it could simply melt her heart. If you wish to create something other than pornography, then you would be well advised to deliver on the second promise.

The third promise is to offer something deeper

This involves giving the reader some intellectual fulfillment: to open her eyes to something she never considered before, or to take her into a strange world that's *full* of things she never considered before. Or it might simply reassure her that things in her own world can work out just fine.

If you aspire to write erotic literature, then you would be well advised to deliver on the third promise.

I have listed the above promises in descending order of importance. The first promise is vital: an erotic tale can be pure arousal, but it must certainly be no less. If you can also deliver the second promise by weaving an entertaining story around the eroticism, then your work will be all the more engaging.

If you manage to deliver on promise number three as well, by bringing out some deeper theme that leaves the reader with an intellectual or emotional response as well as a physical one, then you might just have created a story that will stand the test of time.

The Narrative Promise

Stories that resonate (whether erotic or not) also set up a fourth promise, one that exists at a higher level than the other three. This promise concerns the shape of the narrative as a whole.

Recall that the reader's hope *'crystalizes into an expectation of what the story will deliver by its end.'* The narrative promise is set up by your beginning. It should be developed in the body of the work and fulfilled by its end. The narrative promise can be implicit:

> *Samantha's sex life had never recovered after the night of her wedding—her husband's accident on the second day of their honeymoon had seen to that.*

This beginning tells the reader how things are for Samantha (her sex life torpedoed by some bizarre honeymoon accident) and implicitly promises that, during the course of this story, we will find out what happened, what effect it had in the marital bed, and perhaps see everything restored to its former glory.

The promise can also be explicit:

> *Siobhan's sex life never really got back on track after her husband's little wedding-night problem—until the day he mentioned that he would be bringing his new boss home for dinner.*

This beginning leaves many details to be filled in, but the reader is left in no doubt about the eventual outcome: with the arrival of the new boss, Siobhan's sex life is somehow going to improve.

So we have two types of narrative promise:

- **Implicit Promises** withhold crucial information. Because of this, they naturally support the development of suspense. The reader might hope that Samantha's sex life will take a turn for the better, but what if it doesn't? The key question is *'What?'*: *What happened to destroy Samantha's sex life? What might happen to improve it?*
- **Explicit Promises** answer the *'What?'* question up-front. The interest then arises from the question, *'How?'*: *How will the arrival of the husband's new boss bring a new lease of life into Siobhan's bedroom?*

69

You might never have deliberately placed either kind of promise in one of your stories, but you've probably done so subconsciously. Like many patterns in storytelling, narrative promises can emerge organically without the author's knowing intent. It's worth paying some attention to this aspect of your work; if you're only vaguely aware that you made a promise at the beginning, how can you be certain you've fulfilled it by the end?

Engines of Eroticism

As we saw in Chapter 3, conflict is at the heart of story. By extension, erotic conflict is at the heart of erotic story. A story based on non-erotic conflict might be sexualized by the inclusion of hot scenes, but it won't truly qualify as erotica. It will be a regular story where the characters happen to have a lot of sex.

Ian Fleming's James Bond, for example, is obsessed with the wooing and bedding of various beautiful women—but the bedroom activity is always incidental to the main story. Bond's conquests may gain him female allies to bolster his gadgets and espionage skills, but if spy master 'M' sent an equally charming agent who also happened to be happily married and monogamous, then the tone of the stories might change but the plots could remain largely the same. The sex scenes might be toned down to a yearning glance and the brush of a hand, or cranked up all the way to eleven, without significantly impacting the through-line.

While we're in espionage territory, let's compare two possible spy storylines (both suitably cheesy, in keeping with the genre):

1. A number of our nation's spies have been killed after their covers were blown, the common factor being that the spies' handlers all attended the same exclusive health spa. Our hero (known for his sophisticated charm, rough good looks and womanizing nature) is dispatched to the spa to find out what is going on. It turns out that one of the masseuses is in the pay of an enemy power whose training gave her a hypnotic touch that places massage subjects into a highly suggestible trance state. The hero exploits his charms to seduce and expose the masseuse. The setting provides many other possible sexual partners and many opportunities for sex scenes—*but no matter how many such interludes are included, this will remain a spiced-up spy story rather than a piece of erotica.*

2. Our womanizing hero stands accused by his superiors of spending too much time chasing skirt and not enough chasing the enemies of his country. He is ordered to check himself into a specialized health spa that promises to help sex-addicts overcome their addiction. Traditional spying complications might lead to espionage sub-plots (the hypnotic masseuse might work at the spa) but the central conflict arises from the spy's sexuality: his career depends on finding a 'cure' to his addiction, yet that cure goes against his own nature. To make things worse, the supposed cure takes place in a setting full of alluring therapists (and any number of attractive, sex-starved patients) meaning that the spy's infiltration and penetration skills might lead to all kinds of destinations.

Of course, there's no reason not to include explicit scenes in stories of the first type, just as there's no reason to suppress the sexual side of a mainstream character. But if you plan to write erotica, rather than spiced-up stories, then you should place sexuality at the heart of the conflict[1]. When you do this, eroticism emerges naturally to become a seamless part of the tale.

---

1   This doesn't mean the conflict must be explicitly sexual. In the second espionage example, the conflict arises from the requirement for the spy *not* to behave sexually.

Sex, Tension and Plot

Never lose sight of the fact that tension is what keeps your reader turning the pages. As a storyteller, you build tension by preventing your characters from getting what they need; you release it by satisfying those needs. If the only thing your character needs is sexual pleasure, then you'll probably satisfy that need (and thus puncture the tension) rather easily.

This leads us back to another difference between stories that are erotic by nature, and stories where the sex is bolted on. If you make your character need something that's associated with sex *but that goes further than sex* then you will create lasting erotic tension.

If you make him need something mundane, then the tension might be just as powerful, but it's hardly sexual.

What might a character in an erotic scenario want, beside the obvious? The only limit is your imagination:

- An illicit lover might want to escape detection
- Romeo and Juliet might want to have cooler parents, or to be able to move to a different country
- A *femme fatale* might want to improve her position
- A porn actor might need to deliver a 'money shot' even though he's not that turned on
- A virgin might want to get through his first sexual experience without making a fool of himself
- A lonely-heart might want there to be something more, the following morning or the following year.

All the above characters enter the bedroom with a sexual (or at least romantic) agenda that goes beyond their immediate carnal desire. The more important you make that agenda, and the greater the consequences of its failure, the more erotic tension you will build.

You will also bring your heroes and heroines to life as human beings, not just as rutting machines. Two characters who meet up, conduct a self-contained sexual transaction and then separate—without really touching one another's lives—are not the stuff from which memorable fiction is made. The interest comes from the deeper impact on the characters, not from the physical transaction they shared.

The fact that people go to bed together means there is *some* kind of relationship to be explored, even if it's only a fleeting one. If the sex scene reaches backward and forward to the rest of the plot chain, then it becomes an integral part of the story and not a stand-alone scene[1].

The more deeply your characters want, the more tension you can build by creating doubt about the fulfillment of those wants. The more erotic tension you build, the more concerned the reader will become for your characters, and the more powerful the final release will be. Anger, frustration, yearning, even desperation or despair—all are part of the erotic experience, and all might have a place in your story.

Erotic Pacing and Point-of-View

All fiction must strive to seduce the reader into continuing past the beginning; as an erotic storyteller you have the opportunity to perform this seduction almost literally. You don't necessarily want to drag your reader straight into the bedroom.

In sex scenes as much as in sex, things are often better taken slowly, giving the characters and reader time to enjoy the journey. That's not to say you can never have a couple who are so crazy for one another that they simply rip each others' clothes off and get straight down to it—if that's who the characters are, then that's what the reader wants to see. More often, though, you'll want to build the heat gradually, lingering on desires, textures, sensations, hopes and emotions.

Similar considerations apply to the sexual pacing of the overall narrative. You may be tempted to 'hook' your reader by launching into a steamy scene on page one—but remember that eroticism emerges from character, so that scene could be stronger if you first spent some time establishing who is who.

If you absolutely must have an early sex scene, consider allowing a minor character to take part, rather than your protagonist. Then you can serve up an enticing appetizer while still building tension around the arrival of the entrée.

---

1   The reader of an erotic work expects plenty of heat, and will not demand that every sex scene be dove-tailed into the story. Even so, you can try to strike a balance; too many sex stories amount to a collection of steamy scenes linked by a tenuous plot. Sex scenes are most memorable when they are an intrinsic part of the story.

A common mistake is to assume that just because something is graphic, it must be sexy. This belief can lead to crude, clinical description that is the hallmark of pornography, not erotica. Instead of inventorying body parts, look at your characters' responses to those body parts. Put yourself inside your hero's head. Which of his partner's physical attributes would the hero dwell on? A handful of detailed traits and responses *that are both specific and fascinating to these particular characters* delivers a bigger erotic payload than a whole library of generic anatomy lessons.

Compare the following two snippets:

> *He trailed his lips across her big, firm breasts and clamped his mouth to her engorged left nipple. Her whole body stiffened. He pulled away for a moment. 'You like that, don't you?'*
> *Her only reply was to push him back against her breast.*

The above snippet is generic and anonymous: it could refer to any stock heterosexual pair. Now try this one:

> *He trailed his lips across her left breast, aiming for the petal-shaped birthmark that nestled close to her armpit. As his mouth clamped against the flaw, her whole body stiffened. He pulled away for a moment. 'I didn't know birthmarks were erogenous.'*
> *Her only reply was to push him back against her breast.*

The second snippet includes specific details of physique, dialogue and response that could only belong to these characters. A key difference arises in the single line of dialogue. In the first version, the line *'You like that, don't you?'* tells us nothing, just as it told the character nothing. He was hardly surprised that she liked it; his words achieve little more than to fill some space on the page.

The second version, *'I didn't know birthmarks were erogenous'* signals a piece of information. One of the characters has just learned something about the other.

The exchange of information, whether voiced, silent or purely chemical, is at the heart of sex. The lights might be out, but it's okay (and usually desirable) for your characters to talk. Don't neglect non-verbal signals, either. Gasps, sighs, tactile sensations, scents and flavors can all play their part.

Sexual Superheroes and Comic Book Worlds

Your reader will only stay immersed in your story as long as she accepts the notion that the world you're portraying is real. This acceptance is often called 'the willing suspension of disbelief'. If your reader thought about the matter, she would know that the story was untrue—so the trick is to keep her from thinking about it. Only then can the reader be pulled in so far that she experiences your story as if it were real.

Delivering a believable fictional experience is difficult at the best of times, but with an erotic tale it can be even trickier—such a tale must attempt to do the same work as any other story, while also creating reasons for plentiful sexual activity, and environments where that activity can proceed unhindered.

One way of tackling this problem is to create a kind of comic book world that's similar to reality in many ways, but that's populated by sexual superheroes and equipped with its own internal rules. In this world, human motivations, responses and social norms differ from our own. To give you a flavor of how things might work, here are some examples:

- Everybody is always horny
- Any human institution will be a hotbed of sexual activity
- Sexual favors are the usual currency for paying debts and obligations.

As settings for erotic stories, comic book worlds have a significant advantage. By putting aside the conventions that would interfere with your characters' sexual exploits, they provide unparalleled freedom to explore and trigger erotic scenes. They lend themselves to an escapist (and commercially successful) form of sex writing, where the delivery of the erotic experience trumps all other considerations. They let you 'get the job done' without spending too much time on the finer points of believability.

One problem with this approach is that it can lead to stories that are internally inconsistent. The stories generally take place in a world much like our own—except when it comes to sex. In reality, if we were all constantly horny and inclined to act on those urges, *everything* would change. Work, friendship, leisure, marriage, society itself—it would all become unrecognizable.

A fictional world where a single constraint has been loosened is like a harp with one out-of-tune string. It can still produce music, but there will be a discordant note, something that doesn't quite fit. Many listeners will neither notice nor care; others will walk out in disgust.

If you find yourself unintentionally creating a comic book world, go back to the central conflict or idea driving your work. Do you have a truly erotic premise, or are you trying to bolt a sexy situation onto something else?

The Sex Was Incredible (No, Really)

As soon as the discerning reader mentally exclaims, *'No way!'*, she's been pulled out of the story. For that moment at least, you've lost her. You might get her back, but keep it up and she'll soon be gone for good.

The need for plausibility extends to the sex act itself. If you're not sure about anatomical details, research the matter. When writing a complex physical sex scene, choreograph the action (mentally, at least) to make sure it's believable. And when you describe the sexual response and orgasm of the opposite sex, don't just make it up—get the scoop from an insider.

In erotic fiction, there is no fixed line to be drawn between the credible and the incredible. You might embrace the comic book world, taking the glibbest of liberties with reality. This can be a highly productive route, because you don't have to spend much time on the internal consistency of your world. If you can deliver compelling erotic experiences in such a world, you should not lack for readers.

Or you might tread a middle path, shading the incredible with the credible and craftily concealing the join.

You might even set your erotic tale in the strictly everyday world, with characters who are no more apt to jump out of their clothes than anybody else. Ordinary people can have extraordinary erotic experiences.

The choices you make, and the goals you wish to achieve, will influence where in the continuum your own work will lie.

Weaving the fantastic into the very fabric of a story can, para-doxically, ease the suspension of disbelief. This is one reason why real comic books work so well: the unreality is part of the premise of the story[1]. Otherwise, how could the characters fly, see through walls, have super strength, or whatever?

The same applies with erotica. If your setting has dragons, then it can credibly include love potions and magically operated chastity belts. If your hero owns a star ship and is friends with a computer that invents dirty jokes, then he could also have any other kind of technology — including a collection of astonishing sex toys.

Soft-core versus Hard-core

Different audiences enjoy and expect different levels of explicit-ness. Consider the tastes of those you hope will read your work, as well as your own preferences, when you decide the type of acts you will portray and the language you will use.

You can change the feel of a story completely by expressing it with different words, emphasis and pacing. Don't assume that a romantic storyline must use soft-core language: the audience for such pieces is perfectly capable of enjoying explicit sex and four-letter words. The reverse is less true, though it's possible to imag-ine the most depraved libertine communicating in the most refined language. As ever, there are no hard-and-fast rules. The important thing is to use a vocabulary that matches what you're trying to achieve. The table opposite shows how word choices can move a story across the soft-core/hard-core continuum.

Your choice of activities and vocabulary is not the only thing that influences the level of explicitness. Spending time inside your characters' heads humanizes your work, leading to a slower, more soft-core feel. Concentrating on blunt physical description is likely to create a more hard-core perception and a faster pace.

Take care with euphemisms (including most of the words in the leftmost table column); they can quickly become risible. Given your likely audience, such words are hardly necessary — unless you're working at the fluffiest, most romantic fringe, or writing a character who would use such language.

---

1   Also, only a handful of characters have super powers; the story emerges from the juxtaposition of super-characters with a normal world.

Softer	⟶			Harder
Make Love	Couple	Screw	Rut	Fuck
Nibble	Lick	Suck	Blow	Eat
Bosom	Breasts	Boobs	Rack	Tits
Sex	Pussy	Slit	Snatch	Cunt
Manhood	Penis	Tool	Prick	Cock
Jewels	Scrotum	Testicles	Stones	Balls
Rosebud	Ring	Anus	Ass	Asshole
Arousal	Wetness	Juice	Jism	Cum
Pearl	Bud	Love-button	Clitoris	Clit
Bliss	Consummation	Climax	Orgasm	Come

We will re-visit the topic of erotic vocabulary in Chapter 5, *Delivering the Goods* and Appendix C: *Erotic Lexicon*.

Taboo Areas

How should you deal with taboo subject areas? If you are writing for mainstream publication, the answer is simple: consult the appropriate submission guidelines. Erotic publishers generally list their no-go areas, which will include at least some of:

- Incest and under-age sex
- Bestiality
- Non-consensual activities
- Degradation of either sex
- Branding or drawing blood
- Constriction of the neck.

These no-nos exist for the legal protection of the publisher, and also because publishers understand their target audience and know that certain types of story will not succeed.

BDSM authors pondering the meaning of 'non-consensual' or 'degradation' might do well to study the publishers' book lists along with their guidelines: a publisher who states *'Consensual Activity Only'* and *'No Degrading Behavior'* might still publish novels full of people being held prisoner, humiliated, and compelled to activities that turn out to be surprisingly enjoyable, once the victims allow themselves to enter into the spirit of the thing.

If you plan to submit your work to a more niche-oriented market, you may have more freedom to explore the exotic along with the erotic. But even ebook publishers have their prohibited areas (though given their lower standards of manuscript vetting, and perhaps because they have less at stake, it's fair to say that some electronic publishers let things slip through that they would claim not to).

Drawing the Line

As we've just seen, erotic writing sometimes brings us to boundaries that we must (if we are ethical writers concerned with the effects of our work) at least ponder. Almost everyone will have subject areas that simply don't interest them, or that gross them out or make them think, *'No, that's just wrong.'*

Take a moment to consider whether it's okay to write stories about:

- Sexual violence?
- Sexual harassment?
- Underage sex or incest?
- Casual sex without a condom?
- Activities that are not safe, sane or consensual?
- Fictional memoirs that are thinly-disguised real ones?

The thinly-disguised fictional memoirs could land a writer or publisher with a libel writ. In some countries, writing about underage sex or other illegal activities could lead to similar problems, as could material that might be viewed as an incitement to violence or hate.

Ultimately, you are the only person who can make a judgement about what is appropriate for you to write or publish. If you hold back, you won't be the first writer ever to self-censor. If you push the boundaries beyond what your society will accept, you won't be the first to break new ground—maybe even as part of a prison work gang ☺

The choices you make must be informed by your ethics, inclinations and local circumstances. The ethical writer will *not* publish work with the intention of doing harm.

What about harmful effects that are inadvertent or beyond your control? To what extent should you consider the potential consequences of your writing before you publish it?

69

It's not just authors exploring sexual or societal taboos that face such questions. You might remember the 'copycat crime' controversy surrounding the movie *Natural Born Killers* (the case against director Oliver Stone was ultimately dismissed). In a similar vein, Stanley Kubrick withdrew his film *A Clockwork Orange* from the United Kingdom after that country saw a number of brutal attacks similar to ones portrayed in the movie; the film was only released in Britain after the director's death.

In today's digital world, to publish a story is to set it free. Once it's gone, you can't recall it or control how it will be used—but you can write it as you wished it to be in the first place. You can control the actions and perceptions of your characters, and decide whether they revel in monstrous acts, or deplore them.

If you find yourself uncomfortable with a disturbing scene that is nevertheless integral to your story, here are some techniques that can help dial down the intensity:

- Give POV to the victim, not the monster. This also makes sound story sense: underdogs are more interesting because their position automatically leads to conflict. Those with power have few problems in achieving their objectives.

- Control the depth of POV. Don't hesitate to pull back at times. The more deeply you inhabit the characters, the more intense the reader's experience.

- If necessary, pull the POV away completely: place a minor character in the scene instead of a major one. The viewpoint character (and by extension the reader) is then reduced to the role of witness. If there's a sense that the protagonist might be next, this can build tension better than throwing her directly to the wolves.

- Cast the monster in the role of the villain, not the hero. Even in a horror story, the impact usually comes from sympathizing with the victim, not from identifying with the monster.

- Ensuring that the monster eventually gets his just desserts can help 'balance the book'.

69

When writing about a taboo area, your best approach is to weave it into an excellent story. Quality fiction of any kind is seldom produced by writers with an axe to grind; the 'storyteller' who attempts to justify, or to evangelize, destroys what he set out to do before he has even begun.

Never lose sight of the goals of erotic storytelling: to arouse, to entertain, to move, and to offer sensual experiences that would be impossible in real life. If you pursue those goals with all the dedication and craft at your disposal, you will not go far wrong. Simplistic work is apt to deliver a simplistic message; deeper work will reveal more.

When it comes down to it, questions about the portrayal of taboos, and whether or where a line should be drawn, cannot be answered by any book. They must be addressed by the writer and her conscience—and also, of course, by her publisher.

Chapter Summary

- The erotic promise is that the story will arouse the reader. Ideally, the reader will also be entertained. Perhaps she will even be moved in some deeper way.

- The narrative promise is an over-arching promise that links the beginning of the story to its end. By the end of the story, the promise of the beginning should have been fulfilled.

- Erotic conflict should be at the heart of an erotic story. It's not simply a case of retro-fitting sexy elements to a mainstream story.

- Pace your stories and sex scenes carefully, allowing time for erotic tension to build.

- Give your characters significant wants and needs that are only indirectly sexual.

- Details and behavior that are specific to your characters are more erotic than generic descriptions and responses that could apply to anybody.

- Entering the minds of your characters is much more powerful than describing what happens to their bodies. Use deep point-of-view to bring the reader into an erotic scene.

- Believability is an important issue. You can either throw caution to the winds and set your story in a comic book world, or you can work a little harder to create a setting with some internal consistency.

- Your choice of themes, style and vocabulary will determine how soft-core or hard-core your story is. Consider the needs of your intended market, as well as your own preferences, in making this choice.

- A number of taboos exist, several of which are to be approached with extreme caution if you hope to find a publisher.

- The ethical writer will consider the possible consequences of her work.

- The best place to write propaganda is in a government department. Attempting to twist an erotic story in some self-serving direction is self-defeating.

5 Delivering the Goods

Despite erotica's reputation for being 'easier' than more mainstream genres, it's at least as difficult to write well in this field as it is in any other. The fact that sexy stories can speak directly to a deep human need might make it less *necessary* to write well, but that's a different matter—and one that has led to a widespread perception that erotic writing equals trashy writing.

In the spirit of changing that perception, this chapter examines the most common pitfalls that can relegate an erotica manuscript to the lowest rung of publication possibilities (or scupper any chance of paid publication at all). It also explains how the erotic writer can overcome or avoid these common problems.

All it takes is the willingness to learn and the diligence to put that learning into practice.

Avoid the Omniscient Point-of-View

The first pitfall for beginning erotica authors is the temptation to write from the omniscient point of view You will recall from Chapter 2 that each narrative viewpoint has its benefits and drawbacks.

The benefits of the omniscient point-of-view are mostly about making life easier for the writer. The drawbacks are that the story and characters are generally less sympathetic and engaging for the reader. As an erotic writer in search of an audience, this is not a trade-off you want to make.

None of that is to say that you shouldn't experiment with an omniscient narrator, or to deny that skilled writers might overcome the limitations of this viewpoint. They might manage to bring out all the seductions, sex scenes, and other erotic stuff that goes on largely inside characters' heads, without ever really *being* inside the characters' heads.

If you're that good, you have already gone far beyond what can be taught by a book.

Deliver Subtle Exposition

Exposition is the process of communicating necessary information to the reader. When handled skillfully, the reader is barely aware she is receiving information. Exposition can be done in one of two main ways:

- Telling
- Showing.

You've almost certainly seen the usual writer's advice to show rather than tell. Stated so baldly, the advice can be a little cryptic, and in any case it's not always applicable: there will be times when you want to tell rather than show.

Here's the fundamental difference:

- When you write a summary or give information directly by talking to the reader, you are telling.

- When you write a scene or give information indirectly through story events, you are showing.

Let's explore the difference further by means of a sample beginning. Our goal is to introduce the hero: Philip Sanders. We'll make Philip tall, fit, and successful. He owns an engineering company. He's a nice guy with a mysterious, adventurous past that has affected him in some way to be explored in the story. In his middle years, Philip hasn't yet met the right woman, despite being interested in finding her.[1]

Telling (Summary)

Philip Sanders was exceptionally tall, and in great physical shape. In his thirty-eighth year, he was also at his professional peak, with his own engineering company and enough income to

---

1   As it stands, this outline beginning could launch us into either an erotic or a romantic tale (not to mention all shades in between). The fully fleshed out story might develop eroticism by exploring the mysterious events of his past—since they are brought out in the beginning, this is part of the story's implicit promise. The hero's dating activities obviously provide further opportunities for erotic scenes and conflict.

indulge a taste for the finer things in life—a taste that had led him to exotic lands and strange adventures.

Philip had been through some hard times in his earlier life, but his shrewd, hard-working nature and easy-going personality had seen him rise above those challenges. His friends saw him as the nice-guy-who-has-everything, but Philip knew that something was missing—something had always been missing—from his seemingly-perfect life: the love of a good woman.

Showing (Scene)

'Another date?' Maria asked.

Philip Sanders flipped his cellphone shut and put it back in his pocket. 'Yes.' He rose to his feet and replaced the chair—custom-built in the company workshops for his six-foot five-inch frame—beneath the oversized, burred oak desk.

Maria flashed him an impudent grin. 'What's that, four different dates in one week? You'll be setting a new record if you're not careful.'

Philip frowned at the girl's lack of respect. At thirty-eight, he was almost old enough to be her father—and wasn't he supposed to be the boss, not to mention the proprietor, of this outfit? He wasn't about to fuss at her, though; that wasn't his way. Impudent or not, Maria was one of the few women, nowadays, whose company he could tolerate for more than a few hours. Her dark complexion and fiery nature reminded him of exotic adventures in far-away places—though Philip knew it was unwise to dwell on those times.

He gestured at the paperwork strewn across the desk. 'Let's deal with this tomorrow. I want to hit the gym before—'

'Before you meet the next applicant for the position of Miss Right,' she finished for him. 'Don't worry, I can wrap this up. You go and have fun, and try to relax for once. Give the poor girl a chance.'

The 'Telling' version is not completely horrible. It achieves several important things:

- It names the protagonist and gives a brief physical sketch.

- It describes his position in life, and a little about where he's come from.

- It hints at his taste for the finer things in life, and his appetite for the exotic and for adventure, thus telling the reader of the kind of experience she has in store if she chooses to follow this character.

- It reveals that he's easy going and that his friends think he's a nice guy.

- Finally, it contrasts the perception of his friends with his own self-perception, and shows what's missing from his life—introducing an objective, and possible conflict.

What about the shortcomings of the 'Telling' version?

- It leaves the reader with the nagging question: *'Who is telling me this stuff?'*

- It invites a second question: *'Why should I care?'* We're generally interested in the lives and stories of people we know, at least a little. If you launch into an infodump about a hero before the reader has even met him, you're liable to make that reader's eyes glaze over. Hold the exposition until you've given her a reason to be interested.

- Nothing happened. If you don't show what happens first, how can the reader be interested in what happens next? Yet that is the very question that will make her turn the page.

Obviously, the second version of the opening was re-worked from the ground up, but what *really* changed?

- Philip is present in the scene, speaking and acting, while the narrator has faded into the background. Events are seen through Philip's eyes, and reported through his internal comments and judgements. The reader gets to meet the character.

- Some information is held back for later, while some is revealed naturally: his name, height, status, and adventurous past. His easy-going nature is shown in his tolerance toward his P.A. He's heading to the gym, indicating that he stays in shape. And he's had several dates that evidently led nowhere, showing that he's searching, unsuccessfully, for the right woman.

- Something extra appears: we invented Maria to give him someone to interact with. Who knows? Maybe Maria will turn out to be the woman for whom he yearns, and who's been right under his nose all of this time. Stranger things have happened in erotic/romantic fiction ☺

- By the end of the scene, the story is moving. The characters say and do stuff. Questions emerge. Why doesn't Philip like to dwell on his past adventures? What does Maria really think of her boss? How is his date going to go? The reader (if she's into this kind of romantic piece) might just be intrigued enough by such questions to turn to page two.

- Writing the summary didn't require much thought at all. The scene took more imagination, more work, and more words.

69

Telling isn't always bad. There will be story events that don't lend themselves to showing, perhaps because they are too mundane or because something similar happens several times during the tale—the reader doesn't want to see the same scene over and over.

Here is a piece of telling that might make sense:

> *Philip stocked his car with provisions. He called Maria to tell her goodbye, then drove the 300 miles to the border. Once across, he headed up into the hills.*

If we were to cast the above summary as a detailed scene, we could show him visiting the store and selecting the needed provisions. He might chat with the store keeper and/or Maria, and then sit in traffic—or speed along an open road with the top down and the wind in his hair. He might have to hunt for his documents at the border crossing, and consult a map to find the best route into the hills.

So, which is better, the three lines of summary or a fully-developed scene? It depends on the significance of the events. If the details are significant, spend the time to write the scene. The most obvious candidate here is Philip's call to Maria; the final decision will depend on how the characters' relationship has developed, and how important the call is.

If you just need to move a character from A to B, or to communicate something that's routine, then summary is usually the way to go. If you're dealing with an event that's important to the character, you should write a scene.

The term 'sex scene' includes that second word for a reason, but even then, if your plot insists that the same couple have similar sex on several occasions, you'll eventually want to move away from scene and toward summary. As far as possible, keep your sex scenes, participants and descriptions varied, so that the problems of repetition and staleness don't arise.

69

Exposition can be difficult to do well; many writers are tempted to seek easy alternatives. A common idea is to smuggle a chunk of naked exposition to the reader by pretending it's part of a scene. Examples of this include:

- Conversations where one character tells another character something they both already know, or that is of no immediate interest to either.

- The deliberate introduction of characters who don't know the background, to add an element of plausibility to the conversations described above.

- Interior monologue where a character dwells on something purely to inform the reader, rather than because he has a reason to think about the subject.

All of the above expositional devices have one thing in common: they saved the writer the effort of inventing a believable way to deliver the information. Some readers will accept such devices; many (including all but the most desperate, barrel-scraping submissions editors) will not.

Write Effective Dialogue

The sexiest thing you can put in your heroine's mouth is a line of well-crafted, character-revealing dialogue. Words are the ultimate expression of eroticism, or of any other aspect of character. They can be smooth, confrontational, coercive, defiant, angry, seductive or chilling. They can evoke mood, tone and desire.

On the face of it, writing dialogue should be easy. After all, it's something we do every day. We speak with other people; they listen, understand our meaning, and reply. If we can just reproduce that on the page we'll be fine, right?

Wrong. Fictional dialogue is completely different from everyday speech. Speech is communication; dialogue is performance. Dialogue is a dramatic shorthand that's terse, fluent, dense with information, and well-suited to the task at hand.

Dialogue is Multi-layered

Depending on how you look at things, you might conclude that the purpose of dialogue is to enable...

1. ...characters to communicate with one another.
2. ...story and character to be communicated to the reader.

The first answer is correct, but also superficial. Look more deeply and you'll see that the second is at least as true. Characters are puppets. They can't actually hear or understand, though you must create the illusion that they do. Craft—including well-crafted dialogue—enables you to sustain that illusion.

Your reader *can* hear and understand. When absorbing dialogue, she perceives (from things like openness, evasiveness, timing, attitude and body language) a subtext that goes deeper than the actual words. Here's an example:

> *'Do you think of me as a passionate woman?' she asked.*
> *'I beg your pardon?'*
> *'You heard what I said.'*
> *He hesitated. 'I'm not sure that—'*
> *'I've always thought of myself that way. You know, the sort of woman who grabs what she wants.' She stepped closer. 'What do you think?'*

If we focus on the literal meaning of the characters' words, this little scene shows nothing more than a woman asking a man for his opinion of her. He doesn't give an answer, so she provides her own.

However, the scene contains a subtext that goes beyond what's said. The woman's question is provocative, and the man's evasive responses suggest something—or at least raise questions—about how he feels. The woman's interruption and body language offer further clues. Would you be surprised if this couple ended up in bed together, or staged a demonstration of the adage that *Hell hath no fury like a woman scorned?*

Dialogue is Fluent

Unlike real speech, dialogue is fluent, punchy and packed with meaning. It's 'better' than speech because you don't have to make it up as you go along. Dialogue shouldn't ramble or veer off onto discursive asides; readers have little patience with *'ums'* and *'ahs'*.

If a character is scatterbrained, you might want to indicate this with a few digressions—but even then, your aim is to reveal the character, not to provide a word-for-word transcript of the conversation he'd have in real life.

Dialogue is Engaging

Dialogue reveals the intelligence and wit of your characters. If you've ever eavesdropped on conversations on the street, you'll know that they are often banal to the point of idiocy. Dialogue should make your reader *want* to eavesdrop.

Dialogue belongs to Characters

Vocabulary, tone and diction should all reflect who the character is. A blue-collar worker will usually speak differently from a professor—unless, perhaps, the worker has a college degree. An excited or tense character speaks differently from one who is calm and relaxed.

Since dialogue originates from within your characters, it follows that the subject under discussion should be one that concerns them. Unless it's of genuine and significant interest, why would they waste time discussing it—and why would your reader want to listen in?

Dialogue is Brief

Long speeches seldom ring true. If one of your characters keeps spouting on for paragraph after paragraph, ask:

- Is he being too wordy? Can the essential information be compressed into a shorter, more powerful statement?
- Are you smuggling exposition into a dialogue scene?
- Have you embarked on a sermon? (An erotic story is not generally the best place for one of these).

If a speech continues for more than three sentences or so, think about giving a line to someone else, even it's just to ask a question or offer a confirmation.

Dialogue is an Element of Story

Dialogue doesn't exist for its own sake. It moves the story: warnings delivered, instructions given, assignments arranged, people chatted-up. In the following segment, two young lovers are trying to break into a mysterious house. By the end of the dialogue, they have got a window open and are committed to going inside:

> 'It's locked,' Mark said.
> Julie swung her flashlight up, illuminating the window casement. 'You have to jiggle it. There you go.'
> The window creaked open, so loud that Mark couldn't help flinching. 'I still say we should go to my place. Mom and Dad are out of town until —'
> 'They didn't take your kid brother, did they? Anyway, I don't believe in ghosts. What are you waiting for?'
> Mark didn't move. 'After you.'
> 'You're making me go first?'
> 'You're the one who doesn't believe in ghosts.'
> Julie played the flashlight around the interior of the room and then clambered onto the window ledge. 'Okay. I'm not scared.'

If you write dialogue 'just to give the characters something to do', think hard about cutting it—or integrating it into the story somehow.

Dialogue is Adversarial

If good dialogue were a tennis match, it would be full of smashes, lobs, passing shots and running saves. Nobody's interested in watching the players—even if they're good friends—engage in a series of gentle 'pat-a-cake' strokes over the net.

In tennis, each player has a conflicting agenda. Dialogue should be the same. Give each speaker a personal agenda and make him pursue it. Here is an earlier dialogue sample again:

> *'Do you think of me as a passionate woman?' she asked.*
> *'I beg your pardon?'*
> *'You heard what I said.'*
> *He hesitated. 'I'm not sure that—'*
> *'I've always thought of myself that way. You know, the sort of woman who grabs what she wants.' She stepped closer. 'What do you think?'*

What agendas might the two characters have had? If they had no agendas, or if their agendas were perfectly aligned, would the scene deliver as much tension? Compare the original with this re-written version:

> *'Do you think of me as a passionate woman?' she asked.*
> *'Yes,' he replied.*
> *'Really?'*
> *'You're the most passionate woman I know.'*
> *'That's how I've always thought of myself. You know, the sort of woman who grabs what she wants.' She stepped closer and grabbed. 'What do you think of that?'*

The characters' agendas are now aligned, removing all traces of conflict. Once the man has made it clear that he wants the same thing as the woman, it's quite credible that she would make a physical move. The previous doubt about his response has evaporated, along with every scrap of tension.

Characters can have opposing agendas without being out-and-out rivals. Lovers and friends compete with one another, too. They tease, boast, score points, play games, and generally try to outdo each other. This is part of what makes them interesting to watch.

Dialogue is Oblique

When character A voices a statement or question to which character B is going to respond, you have two options for that response:

- Character B can address the point directly
- Character B can answer obliquely, or not address character A's point at all.

We saw this in the earlier sample that showed Julie and Mark breaking into the mysterious house:

> [Julie]   *'You're making me go first?'*
> [Mark]   *'You're the one who doesn't believe in ghosts.'*

For comparison, here's the direct answer:

> [Julie]   *'You're making me go first?'*
> [Mark]   *'Yes.'*

The direct version does the same job within the scene (Mark makes Julie climb through the open window first) but it's not a satisfactory substitute. The oblique answer delivers more information and raises the tension between the characters (and therefore, for the reader).

In the above exchange, Mark's oblique response provided an implicit answer (*'Yes, I'm making you go first'*), but this needn't be the case:

> *'Are you going to let us go?' Julie demanded. 'Just tell me what I have to do to get out of this place.'*
> *The house's laughter was like wind in ancient chimneys. Then came its words: a whisper caught in the creaking of wood and stone. 'This way.'*
> *The door at the end of the hallway slammed open.*

The house responded, but it didn't answer. Tension thrives on unanswered questions.

Dialogue contains more than Words

Beside portraying verbal communication between characters, dialogue has some other tasks to perform. It should:

- Help the reader keep track of which character is speaking
- Portray the characters' emotions and moods
- Allow the reader to visualize the scene.

The simplest way to identify the current speaker is to use a tag such as *'said'* or *'replied'*. It's not necessary to tag every line; with two speakers, an occasional reminder is all the reader needs.

Some beginning writers go further, trying to wring extra service out of their dialogue tags:

> *'That hurt!' he winced.*
> *'Good,' she gritted. 'You deserved it.'*
> *'It's not fair!' he scowled.*
> *'I'm the one who gets to decide what's fair,' she chuckled.*

Leaving aside the fact that nobody can wince a line of speech (or laugh, smile or quip it, for that matter), these tags are distracting. Unlike the almost colorless *'said'*, they do not fade into the background. They jump out at the reader and draw his attention away from the action of the scene.

The majority of your tags should be *'said'*. Tags like *'replied'* and *'answered'* are also neutral, but don't overuse them in a single segment of dialogue. If appropriate, you can have your characters shout or whisper—but don't overdo it. Once you've established that the tone of the scene includes bellowing, you probably don't need to mention it again.

Here are some more examples that arguably lie in the middle ground:

> *'Be silent!' she hissed.*
> *'Mmmmm,' he moaned.*
> *'Silence!' she commanded again. 'As a lesson, I'm going to leave you like this for another three hours.'*
> *'Damn, I wish I'd emptied my bladder before we got started,' he grumbled.*

Proximity makes the tags more distracting than they would be if used in isolation, but they at least make logical sense:

- *'She hissed'* suggests that she drew out the *'s'* in *'silent'* (it wouldn't work if she'd said *'Be quiet!'*)
- *'He moaned'* is clearly better than *'he said'* when referring to a muffled noise rather than to speech.
- *'She commanded'* reflects the power of her words, adding color to an erotic scene.
- *'He grumbled'* works because grumbling is speech and reflects exactly what he was doing.

Even allowing for the above rationalizations, colorful tags should be the exception rather than the rule. Use them sparingly and only when you can justify them. Having used such a tag, wait a decent interval before using it again.

None of the above means that your characters shouldn't wince, grit their teeth, scowl or chuckle during dialogue. The trick is to separate it out from the speech:

> *He winced. 'That hurt!'*
> *'Good. You deserved it.'*
> *'It's not fair!'*
> *She chuckled. 'I'm the one who gets to decide what's fair.'*

Note how the actions are placed in separate sentences: they accompany the speech but are not an integral part of it.

These minor actions (often referred to as *beats*) have rid the exchange of dialogue tags altogether: the action identifies the speaker. This is particularly valuable in dialogue with more than two participants, where judicious use of beats can help identify who is speaking without resorting to a *'said'* tag on every line. Well-judged beats also help the reader visualize the characters, drawing him into the scene.

When introducing beats into dialogue, use varied expressions, body language and gestures. It's all too easy to fall back on a few staples such as sipping coffee, leaning forward, nodding, smiling, or stubbing out cigarettes.

Always Think Twice (at least)

Recall the sample scene on page 77 between Philip (the reluctantly single owner of the engineering firm) and Maria (his personal assistant). While discussing this scene, I said:

> *Who knows? Maybe Maria will turn out to be the woman for whom he yearns, and who's been right under his nose all of this time. Stranger things have happened in erotic/romantic fiction* ☺

I'm guessing you weren't surprised by this suggestion. If you thought it sounded clichéd, you were right—it was the first thing that came into my head. It's a romantic idea that's been expressed time and again in our popular culture. Readers are steeped in that culture, too, so they are hardly likely to see the idea as a fresh and original one.

That's not to say the proposed story line couldn't work. It depends on how the piece was developed; the writer might set things up so that the reader expects a different outcome, with Maria and Philip coming (as it were) into their own at the story's climax.

Or the writer could think of something completely different.

The point is that the first idea that pops into your head will almost always be the obvious one. Examine your ideas carefully and reject them if necessary. Look for another idea, and another—and examine those carefully, too.

Choose your Words Wisely

The writer who has decided not to settle for producing hackwork will devote significant effort to seeking the best words for the task at hand. When the same type of scene crops up repeatedly in a story, it can be challenging for the writer to deliver fresh words, and thus a fresh experience, every time.

Of course, you need to vary activities from scene to scene. Variety is the spice of lust as well as of life, and readers don't want to see the same activities performed over and again.

Within each scene, though, you still face the problem of how to describe things in a way that's not going to seem stale to the reader. Your first instinct might be to turn to an erotic thesaurus. While such a thesaurus focuses on erotic language more deeply than a regular thesaurus, the additions are often slang-based or historical, and may not offer much that's usable in a contemporary erotic story.

Consider the following exotic synonyms for the word 'abdomen': *Aunt Nelly, Maconochie,* and *Ned Kelly.* Would your readers even understand these words? Would they find them arousing or simply amusing? Would you be better off using contemporary vocabulary like *'Belly'*, *'Abs'*, or *'Midriff'*?

Seeking rarefied synonyms for, say, breasts or genitalia, leads to the same problem: a host of slang and archaic words, many of which will only work if you're writing to a period style[1], or are aiming for humor or pastiche.

So where does this leave you?

The first thing to understand is that there is always at least a handful of words you can use for any given part of the anatomy and any particular activity. I bet you can come up with several words for 'penis' or 'breasts' without too much thought. See Appendix C, *Erotic Lexicon,* if you need some ideas.

Don't overlook the generic terms that can stand in for many different parts of the body, while still being evocative and descriptive. Returning to our attempt to seek a synonym for abdomen:

> *His hand brushed her belly and he trailed his fingers down along the taut, elegant curve of flesh, working his way towards...*

You get the idea. Curves, planes, muscles, skin, flesh, tendons, hollows, clefts, mounds... all these and more are flexible words that can apply to a wide range of anatomy, providing a useful extension to the stock of nouns that are available to describe your characters' bodies.

Taking things a step further—and this should only be done sparingly—some writers press modified adjectives into service. *His hardness. Her wetness.* This only works with a particularly romantic or flowery type of erotica—and whatever the style of writing, it comes across as euphemistic. If you use this approach, keep it under control: it can quickly become risible.

---

1   Historical vocabulary is useful in period erotica, but you should still pay attention to the impact of the words on the modern reader. Some choices will add period color. Others might seem distracting or comical.

Don't reject purely anatomical terms out-of-hand. Some might transport you (and your readers) straight back to biology class, but others can work depending on the tone of the piece and the sophistication of the viewpoint character.

69

Used with care, the vocabulary-extending techniques discussed above should be more than enough to carry a scene or three—and it's fine to re-use the same words in later scenes (they only linger in the reader's short-term memory for a page or so).

Which brings me to the psychological reason for varying your vocabulary in the first place: readers get bored by seeing a term used repeatedly. Reading a fresh, apt and original phrase or word triggers a pleasurable response (though the casual reader may not be conscious of it).

If the term is re-used too soon, that response is reduced—as if the reader's brain has been desensitized to it. After a few paragraphs or pages, the term will be gone from the reader's short-term memory and can be used again without provoking a subconscious reaction of boredom.

So, the first thing to understand is that you don't need to worry too much about finding virgin vocabulary for each scene. The important thing is to have fresh scenes to describe—after all, if the sex in your story is a succession of *they went to bed and fucked in the missionary position* scenarios, your reader is going to lose interest no matter how much linguistic virtuosity you bring to your descriptions.

Sometimes it may be appropriate to short-circuit this word-hunt entirely. Consider what goes on in your own mind when you make love. If you're a straight woman, do you take the time to think '*His dick is inside my pussy*' or does the more primal and urgent '*He's inside me*' come closer to expressing what you feel? (Everybody else: please re-phrase the question to suit whomever you are).

Assuming you chose the shorter answer, isn't it credible that your characters would experience those sensations in the more direct way, too? And that your readers, if you've managed to draw them into your characters' lives and heads, will respond all the more strongly for it?

I'm not advocating that you never write a line like:

> *His engorged cock slid past the warm, welcoming entrance*
> *of her sex*

Rather, I'm saying that you can add a whole new layer of power and variety to your erotic writing if you describe the internal emotions and sensations your characters feel, as opposed to hunting down a collection of increasingly exotic verbs, nouns and phrases to describe the clinical details.

69

Before we leave this topic, I want to discuss an idea that's common in mainstream writing: that descriptive modifiers are invariably weak, and that you should seek a stronger verb or noun and forego the adverb or adjective.

In case you're not familiar with this idea, here are some examples:

Weak	Stronger
He ran quickly after her	He sprinted after her
She rubbed him firmly	She massaged him
They talked under their breaths	They whispered
He looked at her lecherously	He ogled her
She looked at him longingly	She gazed at him
I stroked her gently	I caressed her
She kissed him deeply	She french-kissed him

The advice to eliminate descriptive words holds a pitfall for the erotic writer: follow it blindly and your sex scenes will seem stark and barren, but ignore it and your work will seem flabby and over-written. It's a matter of finding the right balance.

Sex appeals to the senses. The reader wants to see things clearly, to be told that a touch is gentle or firm, that skin is smooth or that muscle is hard or that a pussy is wet. This doesn't excuse weak writing. Find the strongest, most appropriate verb or noun and *then* embellish it with necessary description.

Outside of a sex scene, the traditional advice holds as much weight as it does for any other genre. In particular, if you eliminate the generic and replace with the specific, your writing will be the stronger for it:

> *I want him to come to my bedroom.*
> *I long for him to seek out my boudoir.*
> *I require that he reports to my quarters.*

The overall sentiment is the same each time, but substituting more specific verbs and nouns brings out different nuances. The first statement is as vanilla as it could be. The second version suggests a romantic tone and a very feminine space. The third suggests a military setting and an authoritarian relationship.

The verbs, too, becomes more shaded with meaning with the replacement of the colorless 'want'. In the second version, the deepness of the want is brought out, while in the third it takes on a peremptory, almost commanding, tone.

Even if the invitation were to the most generic of bedrooms imaginable—a rented room in a hotel—choosing the more specific term (*'hotel room'*, or perhaps *'suite'* if the story supports that suggestion of opulence) makes that detail clear and endows the writing with more expressive power.

Crutch Words

Before I leave the topic of word choice, I want to discuss the idea of 'crutch' words and to explain why they can be bad. Crutch words have nothing to do with the groin area; they are words that a writer turns to, time and again, as a crutch to support his writing.

A reliable and impartial way of unmasking any crutch words is to perform a frequency count on your text. At the time of writing, a web frequency indexer exists at:

```
http://www.georgetown.edu/faculty/
   ballc/webtools/web_freqs.html
```

Or simply enter 'Web Frequency Indexer' into your favorite search engine.

If you perform this analysis and find a word like *'Suddenly'* or *'Finally'* at the top of the list, you may be leaning on a crutch word. Does every use of *'Suddenly'*, for example, really reflect a change whose suddenness was worth mentioning? Were the characters really surprised—or were you subconsciously attempting to perk up some mundane event by implying it was unexpected?

Chapter Summary

- Avoid the Omniscient Point-of-View except for experimental work or unless you're unusually sure of yourself. For the erotic writer, its drawbacks almost always outweigh its benefits.

- Don't tell when it's more appropriate to show. Readers like to follow the story by watching scenes, not by being led by the hand. Relegate telling to cases where showing would be inappropriate—when the characters perform a tedious or routine action, for example, or when the action is similar to something that has happened before.

- Write dialogue that is multi-layered, fluent, engaging, character-based, brief, integrated into the story, adversarial, oblique, and that contains more than the words themselves.

- Don't accept the first idea that pops into your head: find something original and unexpected.

- Use a variety of words and phrases to explore erotic situations. Consult a thesaurus if necessary.

- Choose strong, specific verbs and nouns. Avoid weak, generic ones.

- Be aware of over-reliance on crutch words to support weak situations and writing.

6 The Final Touch

Given that you're reading a book on how to write erotic fiction, it's a fair bet that you'd like to reach a wider audience. You might even hope to make some money from your work. Both goals are possible, though neither is easy. Both involve some kind of publication.

Publication always involves giving up rights. If you sign with a publisher, you will be granting them an exclusive right to publish and sell your work, generally for some specified period and in return for payment. By simply posting your work on the internet, you may not be surrendering any formal rights, but you certainly lose a great deal of control over how your story is copied and used.

No matter how you go about making your stories available to others, you need to understand what you're giving up in that process, what you're likely to get in return, and what you really wanted in the first place. *What is your goal?*

For some, the answer is that they wish to sign with a commercial publisher, for whatever kudos or cash that might bring. Others enjoy sharing their work and receiving feedback from appreciative (or constructively critical) readers. Increasingly, writers are looking to get their work into print even if they must pay to do so. The remainder of this chapter discusses each of these goals in turn.

Doing It for Money

Sadly, if you're setting out to establish an erotic writing career that can take the place of your day job, you're likely to be disappointed.

The same could be said of a similar aspiration in any fiction field, of course, but at least in other areas there's the *possibility* of the big advances, movie rights or multi-book deals that can give an emerging author the financial breathing space he needs to take the occupation up full-time.

Mainstream trade publishers lose money on many of their new writers, but they have enough successes to survive, and a few megahits that are virtual money-mints. This explains how they can afford the astonishing advances offered to some new writers—if nothing else, a big advance generates hype: *'If she got a six-figure advance, her book must be really good…'*

The advance proves to everybody concerned that the publisher is serious about this title, and will lavish the attention and marketing money on it that can help it succeed. Book chains (who largely control the retail end of the market) like to see this kind of commitment when deciding which titles to stock and how many copies to order.

A few lucky mainstream authors will receive this star treatment, but the erotic market is pretty well excluded from the gravy train. No matter how great it is, your BDSM opus will never figure as next summer's must-see family movie, or be featured on *Oprah.* Lacking the revenue that would come from an occasional blockbuster success, erotica publishers must cut their coats accordingly. Any advance will be modest; many erotica markets don't offer an advance at all.

69

Let's play with some notional numbers. Imagine that an author has just sold her first erotic novel with the following terms:

- The publisher pays the author an advance of $2000
- The novel's cover price is set at $7.99
- The contract stipulates an 8% royalty on sales, or 64c per copy.

The word *'advance'* means exactly what it says: it's an advance on royalties. Having paid the author up-front, the publisher owes nothing more until the book has sold enough copies to earn out the advance. In this case, the novel must sell 3,125 copies before the author starts receiving royalty checks. Then she will earn $0.64 for every additional copy sold.

If the title fails to sell 3,125 copies then the publisher winds up out-of-pocket and the author receives no further royalties from this book (and quite possibly, no more offers from this publisher).

This is hardly the stuff on which retirement dreams are built. R.W.A. (Romance Writers of America) member Brenda Hiatt[1] collates anonymous earnings reports on her *'Show me the Money!'* web page. The page includes entries for various publishers, along with the average advance, royalty percentage and earn-out (the total figure the author earned from all sales). By its nature, the survey is hardly scientific, but it still makes instructive reading. A couple of highlights:

- The publisher achieving the highest average earn-out (at the time of writing) was Avon/HarperCollins, at $26,000.
- The lowest earn-out was $65, from a niche e-publisher.

Given its origins and intended audience, the *'Show me the Money'* list is slanted toward the romance end of the market[2]. Nevertheless, some of the publishers represent potential markets for erotica or romantica authors—Ellora's Cave and Renaissance Ebooks, for example. The romance and erotica genres have much in common, increasingly so as romance becomes spicier and more daring.

If you still believe that being an erotic author is an easy route to riches, consider the following quote from Black Lace's 2006-7 submission guidelines: *'You cannot earn a living writing for Black Lace.'* It doesn't get more basic, or more honest, than that.

69

There's a positive side to all this. A competent erotica writer can at least make *some* money by selling her work through niche or online outlets. Try that as a writer of thrillers, mysteries or general fiction, where the demand is less primal and where readers are well-served by the mainstream publishing industry.

If you produce a large body of quality work, you might even build up a useful steady income—provided you can keep your titles in print and available to be ordered. A mainstream publisher is unlikely to be of much help here, because:

1   Brenda Hiatt's web site is at: http://www.brendahiatt.com/

2   Romantic fiction is more widely read than erotic fiction, so there's more money available. Even so, romantic authors are plainly not, by and large, getting rich from their work.

- Their royalty rates are too low: back-list sales tend to come in a trickle rather than a flood, so you want to earn dollars, rather than cents, on every sale.

- They are inclined to let older books go out of print. Even if stock remains in their warehouse, declining sales eventually mean the books will be destroyed.

Provided your publishing contract has a proper rights-reversion clause, an out-of-print work should come back under your control to be exploited as you wish. In the age of the internet and of affordable small volume publishing, rights-reverted works can receive a new lease of life.

69

The above hasn't even touched on the difficulty of securing a trade publishing deal in the first place. The major erotic publishers are seeking specific types of material (this goes beyond the taboo-based limits mentioned in Chapter 4; they know their target readership and they understand what will sell).

They also have limited publication slots each year, and a line-up of proven authors who are able to fill many of those slots. If you hope to make a deal with one of these publishers, you must read their guidelines carefully, study several of their published books, and then deliver something that's familiar enough to stay within the publisher's commercial comfort zone—but also fresh enough to blow the submissions editor away.

Judging by their guidelines, some trade erotica publishers seem to be taking qualities such as character and plot development more seriously than in previous years. In one set of guidelines I studied while researching this book, I noticed a palpable sense of regret that previous titles may not have been all the editors would have wished. Time will tell if this attitude turns into something more than words, but it's an encouraging sign for erotica writers who wish to focus on storytelling as much as on smut.

Failure to secure a deal with a big paperback publisher is not necessarily a reflection on the quality of your work (arguably, the best erotic writing is to be found away from the commercial pressures faced by these companies). Don't overlook small presses or e-publishers—but do some research before submitting. Make sure you're happy with the publisher's offerings, including the covers. Track down the books in stores or online, so you can assess how readily they're available. If your potential publisher's paperbacks are not in stock, will your local bookstore order them? What about the physical quality of the books? Purchase a sample and check it out. Be wary of any publisher who promises that success will come easily, or that they have a magical solution to the problem of getting published and read.

In the case of ebooks, find out how many formats are supported and how many retail sites offer the books. Ebook distribution is highly fragmented. If an e-publisher wants to list on Amazon, for example, she must create a special seller's account and upload her books directly. The same goes for several other websites. An e-publisher that covers fewer retail bases will make fewer sales.

Some paperback publishers will not consider works where the electronic rights have already been sold, so approach e-publication with caution if you also hope for print publication.

Always check which rights the publisher wants. Some publishers make a rights-grab, snapping up as much as possible in the hope it will turn out to be valuable. Even if you never expect your work to appear in French or Chinese, or to be made into an audiobook or movie, why assign these rights to a publisher who can't exploit them? (Unless the company has a track record in selling those rights and sharing the benefit with authors, of course).

For publishers with books listed on Amazon.com, the website's *'Advanced Search'* facility is a useful research tool. Enter the publisher's name and leave all the other fields blank. You will then be able to view the sales ranks, reader feedback and availability of their titles. If most of the books are unavailable, unlamented and ranked below three million, that's an indication of the likely fate of your own work should you send it to the same place.

69

As an erotica writer, you're unlikely to secure the services of a reputable agent (unless you also work in a more profitable genre). Literary agents make their living by taking a percentage of the author's earnings: the possibility of receiving 15% of a $2,000 advance isn't likely to tempt them—and neither is the prospect of being snowed under by submissions from hordes of would-be erotica writers.

The positive side of this is that, in contrast with much of the industry, publishers in this genre are happy to receive unagented submissions—and of course, if you land a deal, you don't have to give up 15% of the proceeds. The drawback is that you don't have a professional on your side whose interests are aligned with yours—the publisher is *not* on the same side as you.

The standard advice must be *'consult a lawyer who specializes in publishing contracts'*—which is an excellent idea as long as you can justify the cost.

If you can't afford professional advice, at least make sure you understand every term of your contract. Educate yourself in the jargon. Seek out sample publishing contracts on the internet and study the explanations that often go with them. Take part in writers' forums (either in the real world or on-line) where you may find experienced professionals willing to advise you (even if they, like myself, include the disclaimer *'I am not a lawyer'*).

Receiving your first publishing contract is a heady experience, but don't let that bounce you into signing a document you don't understand. Research the publisher (as usual, search engines are your friend). Consider all the implications and identify what's important to you. Seek out horror stories from authors who couldn't get their rights back when their publisher went bust, or who never received a single royalty check, or whose publisher scattered typos across the author's carefully-prepared manuscript.

The chances are that any publishing misstep you're about to take has already been regretted by someone else—and that they've documented it on a web forum somewhere.

Giving It Away
Don't hold your breath expecting anyone other than your fellow erotic readers and writers to recognize your achievements in this field—and with them, what counts is producing excellent work and getting it into places where it can be read.

When setting out to get noticed, publishing, rather than payment or prestige, is the name of the game. A lowly e-book deal can gain readers who will later buy your paperbacks. Posting your work for free on the internet can build a following that later flocks to your first commercially-published novel—leading to a rush of sales right off the block that will astound and delight your publisher. Commercial publishers will take you more seriously if you can point to a significant reader base—and as a switched-on erotica writer working in the internet age, you're well-placed to achieve that.

Don't assume that readers will accept something just because it's free, though. You might be offering a free story, but you're asking for something more valuable in return: your readers' attention. Your story had better be worth their time if they're to finish it, or come back for another, or remember your name.

If you want to build a reputation through offering free erotic stories, you must find a way to connect with readers. Buying a domain name and setting up a web site is a good start, but you still have to persuade people to visit the site and read the stories. To be effective, an author's web site should be part of a bigger promotional program.

You can take advantage of existing web sites that host erotic stories, and/or that provide forums for posting and discussing them. Here's how to find the best web sites for the type of fiction you write:

1. Imagine the search words someone would use if they wanted to read a story like yours.
2. Enter those words into your favorite search engine.
3. Click through to the listed web sites. You're looking for the ones that have discussion forums, critique groups, or areas where you can post your work.

Don't overlook other nooks and crannies, such as Usenet news groups or mailing lists that cover erotic fiction. Here are a couple of online resources devoted to the erotic writer:

```
http://www.erotica-readers.com
http://www.asstr.org/
```

It might seem that publishing your stories without payment is less of a commitment than signing a contract with a publisher, but you shouldn't underestimate the possible effect of any publishing decision. You still need to balance what you're giving up against what you hope to gain.

By posting your work in a public forum, you may be surrendering your first-publication rights (which are often the only rights a publisher will consider buying). Sharing your work in a closed forum (a private email list, for example) might be safer, but every publisher has its own set of rules.

Even if you have no intention of submitting a piece to a publisher, once you've sent it out electronically you've lost control over what happens to it: the work can be copied, shared and even stolen. The Usenet news group `alt.sex.stories.d` features regular complaints by writers who have posted their erotic work, only to see it pirated and sold.

Which takes us back to the original point: when you publish, you inevitably give something up. As long as you understand the trade-off you're making, there shouldn't be a problem.

Paying for It

Before paying to have your work published, at least try to place it with a commercial publisher who:

- Bears all the costs of publication
- Vets manuscripts for quality
- Applies a professional level of editorial and design skill
- Pays a royalty on each copy sold
- Relies on sales to the public, rather than to the author.

Desirable as it might be, commercial publication is difficult to achieve. Frankly, most works fail because they're not very good, but quality submissions get turned down too. Perhaps a story was too experimental, or its theme approached too closely to some taboo. Perhaps it just wasn't quite what the publisher was looking for that day.

It's also possible for an author with a contract in her hand to look at the terms and think, *'I can do better than that by going it alone'*.

Presuming you can't or won't secure a commercial publishing contract but are still determined to see your book in print, it may be time to consider some kind of non-commercial or independent publishing. Be clear about your motivation when embarking on this course: do you want the satisfaction of holding a printed and bound volume of your work, and maybe of giving a few signed copies away, or are you hoping to turn a profit? If the latter, don't kid yourself that it's going to be easy:

- If publishers have rejected your work because it's not good enough to sell, then *it's not going to sell—period.*
- If publishers have rejected your work because it wasn't suitable for their needs—and in spite of its high quality—then you might succeed in selling it *if you work hard and get lucky.*

How do you tell if your work is any good? Your first clue might come from rejection notes—erotic editors can be surprisingly generous with their time, and if you're lucky enough to receive their thoughts on your manuscript then you should treat that advice like gold dust.

To set up a paperback for printing requires a significant investment in editing, page layout and design work by many skilled professionals. By contrast, an ebook can be formatted (given the right software) in a few minutes, and uploaded for sale just as quickly. Unburdened by hefty title set-up costs, e-publishers can accept books that wouldn't work in paperback: even if an ebook only generates $20 of profit in a year, that's $20 the e-publisher wouldn't have otherwise had. A paperback that generates just $20 would be a financial disaster.

This means that e-publishers can adopt a *'pile them high and sell them cheap'* approach, without being too fussy about quality or too narrow in their requirements. If you submit to several e-publishers and are rejected by all of them—well, let's just say it's a kind of feedback.

Also try to get your work into the hands of impartial reviewers (*not* your boyfriend, girlfriend or spouse) and be prepared to listen to their critiques. Real-world groups or workshops for erotic writers might be thin on the ground, but there are plenty of suitable online forums. The more you put into such a group, the more you're likely to get out of it—as long as the membership is focused on mutual improvement, rather than on mutual masturbation.

Offset Printing versus Print-on-Demand

The most fundamental decision facing the independent print publisher is the method of book production:

- An old-style printing business uses offset printing presses. These presses use plates that are etched with the images and text that make up the book. Preparing these plates, and setting up the print job, is time-consuming and expensive. Once the set-up work is done, however, books can be printed quite economically. Economies of scale apply: the per-book cost for a run of 500 copies will be significantly more than for a run of 5,000 copies.

- A new breed of print-on-demand (POD) businesses use digital presses. The book is stored as a set of computer files, and printed in batches as small as one. The so-called presses have more in common with laser printers than with the old-style offset presses. Because the set-up work is reduced (there's no need to etch printing plates or to manually set up a print job), the initial investment is much lower. However, digital printing offers no economies of scale: if it costs $5 to produce one copy of your book, it will generally cost $5,000 to produce 1,000 copies (and you'd take your order for 1,000 to an offset printer instead).

If you are confident of selling thousands of copies of your work, and don't mind managing the inventory and distribution headaches, an offset run will deliver the maximum return. The books will cost you less, meaning you can lower your prices and/or make more profit on each book you sell.

For the emerging writer who can't be confident of selling large numbers of books—and for anybody on a tight budget or who doesn't want to risk ending up with a garage full of moldering cartons—print-on-demand is the safer choice.

Assuming you decide to independently publish your erotic work in POD form, you still face a number of challenges:

- Fee-based POD providers are little more than vanity presses, with hefty charges that most authors will never recoup.

- Vanity books are often listed at retail prices that are hard to justify, compared to the competition.

- The same problem applies if the author tries to sell his own work: the high base price charged by the vanity press means that the author must either take a minuscule profit, or set an inflated price.

- Certain vanity presses will not deal with erotica[1].

- Many vanity-published books are poorly written and edited. Vanity presses have no incentive to produce quality work, since their income comes from fee-paying authors rather than from book sales to the public.

- Bookstores generally don't stock POD books.

- Certain bookstores will not even order the offerings of some vanity presses, because of the questionable quality and whole-sale terms offered by those companies.

Be very sure of what you're getting into before surrendering your work to the clutches of a vanity publisher. What are the fees? How will your book be priced? Will the cover be any good? How many copies will you have to sell to recoup your costs? Do they take any rights, and if so under what circumstances can you re-claim them?

At least one vanity POD outfit masquerades as a commercial publisher. They don't charge money up-front, but they also don't sell books to the public. Instead, they pressure authors into buying consignments of their own books at highly inflated prices.

You have potent tools at your disposal for detecting such scams and for finding the best companies. Investigate the company's titles on Amazon, and don't forget the power of the search engine for performing background checks.

Above all, stay realistic in your expectations. Don't invest in book production without understanding how difficult it might be to recoup your costs.

---

1   Given the other drawbacks, this is not necessarily a bad thing.

Chapter Summary

- The most important thing when considering how to publish your work is to be clear on what you wish to achieve.

- Have realistic expectations. You're not going to make a million dollars from writing sexy stories.

- Trade publication might be seen as the most prestigious form of erotic publication, however it means conforming to a strict, arguably formulaic, set of guidelines. Even then, the chances of success are slim, while publishers' response times are lengthy.

- Publishing with a small press or an electronic publisher can be a viable alternative. They may not pay as much—but no erotic publishing deal is likely to secure your next yacht.

- Offering your work for free can gain you valuable exposure, as long as your stories and promotional efforts are good enough to be noticed in a crowded marketplace.

- Various forms of independent publishing offer an alternative for those determined to see their work in print, but vanity-published books are unlikely to earn back their costs.

Appendix A
Erotica, Literature and Commercialism

Erotica versus Pornography

The central intention of this book has been to promote erotic storytelling rather than sex-driven pornography. I have argued that erotica must offer something more than pornography: both forms set out to arouse, but erotica goes further and requires more work from the writer.

The following table summarizes the differences:

Erotica	Pornography
About characters who have sex	About the sex had by characters
Reader identifies with characters' emotions and dilemmas	Reader identifies with characters' arousal and sexuality
Subtle, romantic, elegant	Down-to-earth, to-the-point, functional
Stimulates erotic sensibility	Stimulates physical release
Appreciated over time	Focuses on the job in hand
Consumes, and consumed by, the mind	Consumes, and consumed by, the body

Literary versus Commercial

At first sight, it might seem that the above table equates erotica with literary writing, and pornography with commercial writing. The truth is more complex: literary novels are often driven by an examination of some aspect of the human condition, while commercial novels are driven by characters and plot.

Take the *Story of O* (already mentioned in Chapter 3, *Plot and Structure*). Despite its enormous commercial success, this is at heart a literary work whose power (once the electrifying opening gives way to the main body of the book) is in its examination of O's nature, and of how she embraces submission to the point of self-annihilation—and even draws a kind of perverse power from that submission.

Many readers find themselves disappointed once that electrifying beginning is over. It's a safe bet to say that they missed the tension, conflict and character engagement found in more commercial stories. In place of conflict, O offers compliance. The idea of resistance is foreign to her: if the only way to win her lover's affection is to be tortured, then tortured she will be—and if he's still not pleased, well, she will be disappointed but she won't try to do anything about it.

That's not a good foundation on which to build tension. If you've read *Story of O*, ask yourself:

- To what extent does its popularity stem from the opening?
- Would it be more or less of a success if the passion of the opening had continued through the middle and end?
- How about if the entire book were written in the style of the middle and end?

Story of O is an iconic work of erotic literature. That doesn't mean you shouldn't study it critically to see which aspects might work—or not—in your own writing. Will you set conflict to the side while you examine some aspect of human sexuality? *Story of O's* lack of rising tension and climactic resolution don't matter because the business of the book is to explore the depths of self-effacement to which a submissive human can aspire.

At the opposite end of the spectrum is one of the few erotic novels I've actually found entertaining: Sarah Fisher's *Captivation*, published by Chimera. The subject is similar to that of *Story of O*: the involuntary induction of a girl into sexual slavery. The journey is measured by similar milestones (collarings, whippings, piercings, and so on).

Unlike the compliant O, however, Alex (the heroine of *Captivation*) is highly conflicted about what's happening to her. She agonises about it, rebels against her own nature, has tantrums and even escapes. She's a heroine in the true sense of the word—and the novel's erotic climax, when it comes, is all the more satisfying for that.

Does this make *Captivation* a better novel than *Story of O?* Of course not. By almost any measure of success—originality, literary depth, beauty of prose, and commercial success in print and other media—*Story of O* outclasses *Captivation*.

Still, many would find *Captivation* to be more gripping. It is a commercial story, not a literary study. It's designed to make the reader keep turning the pages, not to pass comment on the human condition. It will never win a major literary price, as did *Story of O* in 1955. It will never be among the first of its kind.

That doesn't mean you shouldn't take a close look at *Captivation* (or similar contemporary works) to see how a skilled commercial author can whip up tension, raise the stakes, and build sympathy for her heroine.

Literary or commercial? It's up to you. What type of story do you prefer to write and to read? What type of readership do you envisage for your work? Whichever you choose, don't be overly constrained by that choice:

- Literary erotica doesn't have to be an introspective plod. Why not offer your readers a serving of tension, of action that rises to a climax, along with your polished prose and your human insights?

- Commercial erotica doesn't have to be a loosely-linked set of bump-and-grind scenes performed by cardboard cutouts. If your characters aren't developed into living, breathing human beings, how can they display a full range of erotic responses?

Appendix B
The Hero's Journey (with pop-culture context)

Act One: Departure	External Journey	Internal Journey
The Call to Adventure	Hero in his mundane world	Hero is suffering from some flaw, often one that prevents him from fulfilling his potential
	Star Wars: Luke Skywalker called to adventure by R2D2's message.	
Refusal of the Call	Hero reluctant to answer call	Flaw or limitation prevents Hero from acting
	Star Wars: Luke held back by sense of own limitation and by family obligation	
Supernatural Aid	Encounters mystical or wise figure who offers guidance/material aid	Hero begins to learn and grow
	Star Wars: Luke receives his father's lightsaber, and spiritual guidance, from Obi-Wan Kenobi	
Crossing the First Threshold	Hero crosses from mundane world into the world of adventure	Hero often passes some test proving worthiness and resolve
	Star Wars: the slaughter of Luke's family pushes him across the threshold into opposing the murderous forces of the Empire	
Rebirth (Belly of the Whale)	Hero engulfed by difficulties and faces a key make-or-break moment	Hero leaves some aspect of self behind and undergoes rebirth or metamorphosis
	Star Wars: in the belly of the Death Star, Luke undergoes pivotal change as he watches Obi-Wan permit himself to be struck down by Darth Vader's lightsaber	

Act Two: Initiation	External Journey	Internal Journey
The Road of Trials	The Hero faces a number of ordeals	The Hero grows as he overcomes the trials
	Empire Strikes Back: Luke and his friends face one setback after another	
Meeting with the Goddess	The Hero encounters a powerful being incorporating symbolic aspects of mother, sister and/or lover	The Hero embraces a previously neglected aspect of himself, gaining mastery over life
	The Matrix: Neo fulfils the prophecy only when he learns that Trinity loves him. Trinity (as suggested by her name) comprises all three aspects of Goddesshood: love interest, sister-in-arms and nurturing mother	
Temptation	The Hero is tempted away from the true path	The Hero struggles with temptation or is repulsed by it, according to his nature
	Empire Strikes Back: Luke tempted by the Dark Side of the Force.	
Atonement with the Father	The Hero encounters some powerful paternalistic figure and there is a reconciliation between them	The Hero experiences 'at-ONE-ment' with the father-figure
	Return of the Jedi: Luke rejects the Dark Side and refuses to kill his father, Darth Vader	
Apotheosis	The Hero overcomes the ultimate challenge	The flaw that prevented the Hero from fulfilling his potential has been resolved
	The Matrix: Neo confronts and defeats Agent Smith	
The Ultimate Boon	A benefit is bestowed on the Hero	The Hero is often motivated to pass the benefit to others
	Return of the Jedi: Luke becomes a true Jedi knight	

Act Three: Return	External Journey	Internal Journey
Refusal of Return	Rather than returning to the mundane world, the Hero may prefer to remain in the world of adventure	Transformed by his experiences, the Hero may no longer wish (or be able) to return to his old life
	Back to the Future: at the end of the movie, Marty McFly chooses to embark on another time adventure rather than immediately returning to his 1980s family life.	
Magic Flight	The Hero may have to flee back to the mundane world	The Hero seeks escape and restoration
	The Matrix: Neo transfers out of the Matrix and back to the Nebuchadnezzar at the last possible moment following his victory over Agent Smith.	
Rescue from Without	The Hero may need to be rescued by a third party.	Pay-off or closure of an earlier part of the story.
	Star Wars: Luke saved by Han Solo during the attack on the Death Star	
Crossing 2nd Threshold	The final return to the mundane world. The Hero may face challenges or gatekeepers.	Reborn to humanity
	Star Wars: Escape from the Death Star and destruction of pursuers	
Master of Two Worlds	The Hero receives his reward	The Hero resolves the conflict between the world of adventure and the mundane world
	Back to the Future: Marty McFly returns to a revised–and much more desirable–version of his previous life.	
Freedom to Live	The Hero has the freedom of both worlds.	The Hero's new knowledge lets him benefit the world
	The Matrix: Neo can enter the Matrix with impunity and has the power to defeat the machines	

Archetype	Purpose	Description and Example
Hero	Sacrifice and service	The protagonist *(Star Wars: Luke Sky-walker)*.
Mentor	Guidance	Offers aid, advice and training to the Hero. May also act as the Hero's conscience *(Star Wars: Obi-Wan Kenobi)*.
Threshold Guardian	Tests	Tests the Hero's worthiness and resolve at key transition points, especially at the Crossing of the First Threshold *(The Matrix: Morpheus offering Neo the red and blue pills)*.
Herald	Challenges and Warnings	Announces the challenge that begins the Journey. The archetype can also be used later in the Journey to signal changes *(Star Wars: R2D2)*.
Shapeshifter	Confusion and Deceit	Has changeable or uncertain loyalties, and can dazzle, confuse, delay or help the Hero *(Star Wars: Han Solo)*.
Shadow	Destruction	The dark or unexpressed side of a character's nature. Villains are often Shadows, but Heroes may also include the Shadow element. *(Star Wars: the Dark Side of the force)*.
Trickster	Disruption	Make mischief and offer light relief. They can trigger change even if they do not change as characters themselves. *(Star Wars: R2D2 and C3PO)*.

The archetypes are not mutually exclusive. The Hero could have a dark (Shadow) side. He might also adopt the role of Trickster or Shapeshifter at certain points.

APPENDIX B: THE HERO'S JOURNEY (WITH POP-CULTURE CONTEXT)   115

The Sensual Journey

If you want to adapt parts of the Hero's Journey for erotic purposes, you might find the following analysis useful:

The Hero's Journey	The Sensual Journey
Call to Adventure	Protagonist receives some romantic or erotic challenge.
Refusal of the Call	Refusal of the challenge.
Supernatural Aid	Protagonist receives erotically-oriented training, clothing, equipment, help, or advice.
Crossing the First Threshold	Passing from the Normal World into the Sensual World.
Rebirth	First significant stirring of the Protagonist's new sexual nature.
The Road of Trials	Thrills, adventures, trials and setbacks
Meeting with the Goddess	Encounter with Protagonist's 'missing other half'—a profoundly life-changing event.
Temptation	May or may not be directly sexual.
Atonement with the Father	Resolution of some sexual or psychological issue, or perhaps atonement for previous temptation.
Apotheosis	Protagonist transcends previous sexual limitations.
The Ultimate Boon	The Ultimate Sex, Ultimate Relationship, or acceptance of the Protagonist's new sexual state.
Refusal of Return	Protagonist refuses to return to innocent state.
Magic Flight	Protagonist may need to flee from antagonist.
Rescue from Without	Protagonist may be rescued.
Crossing 2nd Threshold	Protagonist comes home to the Normal World...
Master of Two Worlds	...while retaining full membership of the Sensual World...
Freedom to Live	...and is thus able to enjoy the benefits of both.

Alasha's Journey: The Sensual Journey in *Property Rites*

When I wrote my BDSM novel *Property Rites*, I had scarcely heard of the Hero's Journey. It was only when searching for erotic examples to illustrate this Appendix that I realized how the structure of my own novel mirrored the Hero's Journey:

The Hero's Journey	Alasha's Journey
Call to Adventure	Newly-orphaned Alasha receives a note from her swindling stepfather. She is now legally his slave.
Refusal of the Call	She refuses to accept her new reality.
Supernatural Aid	She is fitted with a chastity belt and other tokens.
Crossing the First Threshold	'Entertained' in the barracks by her stepfather's soldiers...
Rebirth	...to Alasha's dismay, a treacherous part of her enjoys it.
The Road of Trials	Transferred to a slave caravan, Alasha embarks on a series of submissive adventures.
Meeting with the Goddess	She encounters a romantic hero—her missing other half.
Temptation	A slave-trader doses Alasha with an aphrodisiac drug.
Atonement with the Father	Corporally punished, Alasha experiences at-ONE-ment.
Apotheosis	Alasha realizes she is free to be a slave, or not.
The Ultimate Boon	Estranged romantic hero offers reconciliation and restoration of status...
Refusal of Return	...but Alasha rejects him.
Magic Flight	Having secured her own independence, Alasha returns home to her stepfather's castle...
Rescue from Without	...only to be captured by her stepfather's men, and then rescued.
Crossing 2nd Threshold	Alasha reclaims the duties and obligations of her old world...
Master of Two Worlds	...but retains her new sensual nature...
Freedom to Live	...and so has the life she wishes.

The correspondence is not 100%, but the fact that it's there at all—in a book that wasn't written to any consciously-understood pattern—shows the pervasive power of the Hero's Journey.

Not every story breaks down into such steps. It's only one of many possible story-shapes; even where it applies, elements will usually be omitted or used in a different order. For example, in *The Matrix*, Neo's Apotheosis is concurrent with his Meeting with the Goddess: Trinity kisses him (while he's unconscious) and tells him she loves him.

The point is to appreciate the mythic elements of this Journey. Humans feel an instinctive resonance when they hear stories containing these elements. For anyone seeking to tell tales, understanding that resonance cannot be a bad thing.

Further Reading

The term 'Hero's Journey' came to prominence in the works of Joseph Campbell, including *The Hero with a Thousand Faces*.

Christopher Vogler's *The Writer's Journey* is a distillation of Campbell's ideas supported by analyses of many contemporary stories.

Appendix C
Erotic Lexicon

By their nature, sex scenes pay close and repeated attention to the physical, which can lead to difficulties in keeping your descriptions fresh and varied.

This Appendix aims to help. The terms within each section are not synonyms—or even the same parts of speech. Rather, each list focuses on a particular area, showing words that *might* be useful in a corresponding description .

The lexicon contains a broad range of terms whose suitability depends on the story you wish to tell. Choose whatever works for you and ignore the rest. Don't neglect your thesaurus—or your own creativity and imagination.

Arousal: agitation, alive, aroused, awakening, craving, electricity, excitement, flushed, greed, horny, hunger, inflamed, longing, heat, kindled, lust, on fire, passion, rosy, sparking, stirring, urge, warmth, wetness, willingness, yearning.

Breasts: areola, boobs, bosom, breasts, bust, chest, cleavage, décolletage, dugs, globes, knockers, mammaries, mounds, nipples, nubbins, rack, teats, titties, tits.

Backside: ass, arse, backside, behind, bottom, bum, buns, butt, butt-cheeks; buttocks, cheeks, derrière, dimples, fundament, globes, haunches, hindquarters, orbs, peaches, posterior, rear, rear-end, rump, seat; anus, asshole, arsehole, butthole, rectum, ring, sphincter.

Cruelty: ache, anguish, beastly, bitter, brutal, callous, cold, cruel, desolation, enraged, feral, ferocious, frenzied, grim, hard-hearted, harsh, heartless, hurtful, inhuman, merciless, murderous, ordeal, pitiless, punishing, rack, relentless, remorseless, rough, ruthless, sadistic, savage, severe, shock, smarting, stark, suffering, torment, torture, unmerciful, unyielding, vicious, woe, wretchedness.

Desirability: agile, allure, athletic, arresting, attractive, beautiful, bonny, bountiful, broad-shouldered, burly, busty, brawny, come-hither, comely, cracking, craggy, delicate, desirable, fair, fetching, feminine, firm, flexible, gentle, good-looking, graceful, handsome, hard, lean, leggy, lithe, lithesome, lissome, lovely, luminous, masculine, manly, muscular, nimble, nubile, petite, pliant, potent, pretty, pumped, radiant, ravishing, ripped, rippling, tender, sexy, shapely, sinewy, slight, slender, slim, smooth, spare, stacked, strapping, striking, stunning, supple, svelte, sylph-like, taut, virile, voluptuous, well-built, well-made, wiry, womanly.

Eroticism: amatory, amorous, aphrodisiac, ardent, arousing, bawdy, carnal, debauched, decadent, depraved, dirty, dissolute, erotic, earthy, erogenous, fervid, fiery, filthy, horny, hot, impassioned, inflammatory, lascivious, lecherous, lewd, libidinous, lubricious, lusty, passionate, prurient, randy, raunchy, raw, ribald, risqué, romantic, salacious, seductive, sensual, sensuous, sexual, spicy, steamy, stimulating, suggestive, titillating, unchaste, venereal, wanton.

Female Characters: babe, baggage, belle, broad, call-girl, chick, concubine, courtesan, dame, Domme, fair sex, gentle sex, girl, girlfriend, handmaiden, harem girl, harlot, houri, Jezebel, lady, lass, lover, maid, maiden, miss, Mistress, scarlet woman, skirt, slave girl, strumpet, trollop, wanton, wench, whore, wife, woman.

Female Genitals: beaver, box, bush, cleft, crease, crevice, crotch, cunny, cunt, folds, honey pot, labia, lips, mons veneris, mound, muff, nether lips, opening, oyster, pussy, quim, secret lips, slit, snatch, twat, vagina, vulva; bud, bump, bundle of nerves, clitoris, jewel, love-button, nub, nubbin, pearl.

Hair: bangs, braid, bristle, cascade, coiffure, corkscrew, curls, down, dreadlocks, fleece, fringe, fuzz, locks, mane, mop, peach-fuzz, pelt, pigtail, plait, ponytail, pubes, pubic hair, strand, stubble, ringlets, shock, stray curl, stray wisp, tangled, thatch, tousled, tresses, tumble, wiry.

Head: bridge of the nose, brow, cheek, cheekbones, chin, cranium, ear[lobe], eyebrows, eyelashes, eyes, face, forehead, hair, lips, mouth, nape, neck, nose, pate, scalp, skull, temple, teeth, tongue.

Limbs (lower): ankle, buttock, calf, hip, kneecap, knee, limb, pegs, pins, shin, thigh, shank; arch, ball-of-the-foot, big toe, clefts, foot, heel, instep, little toe, sole, tiptoe, toe, toe-cleft, toenail.

Limbs (upper): armpit, arms, biceps, crook of the arm, elbow, forearm, hand, limb, triceps, shoulder, upper arm, wrist; finger, fingernail, fingertips, fist, forefinger, hand, heel, index finger, knuckles, little finger, middle finger, open hand, palm, ring finger, thumb, wrist.

Love Nests: apartment, bedchamber, bedclothes, bedframe, bedroom, bedspread, bedstead, blanket, bolsters, boudoir, bower, cell, chalet, chamber, comforter, counterpane, couch, duvet, eider-down, four-poster, hideaway, hotel room, lodge, love nest, mattress, pad, penthouse, pied à terre, pillows, quilt, sack, sheet, suite, waterbed.

Male Characters: beau, blade, bloke, bounder, boy, boyfriend, cad, Casanova, chap, cuckold, debaucher, Dom, Don Juan, eunuch, fellow, gigolo, goat, guy, husband, lad, lady's man, ladykiller, lecher, letch, libertine, Lothario, lover, man, Master, rake, rakehell, roué, philanderer, satyr, slave boy, stud, womanizer.

Male Genitals: bone, boner, bulb, cock, crown, dick, erection, glans, hard-on, head, helmet, manhood, knob, meat, member, organ, pecker, penis, phallus, pizzle, pole, prick, rod, sex, shaft, tool, wood; balls, bollocks, crown jewels, family jewels, gonads, nuts, rocks, sack, scrotum, stones, testes, testicles.

Nakedness: bare, barefoot, butt naked, disrobed, exposed, in the buff, naked, nude, stark naked, stripped, unclothed, uncovered, undraped, undressed, unshod, unwrapped, without a stitch.

Orgasm: bliss, climax, come, consummation, cream, culmination, cum, ejaculation, emission, fulfilment, get off, money-shot, peak, rapture, release, relief, satisfaction, shoot, spend, spurt, squirt.

Physical Actions: assail, assault, attack, bear down, bend, compel, caress, cup, drive, embrace, enforce, engulf, explore, force, impale, impel, invade, kiss, lick, lie, lunge, lurch, open, part, penetrate, plow, plunge, poke, possess, press, prod, prostrate, ram, roam, shove, spread, squat, stroke, suck, thrust, tongue, transfix, urge.

Physical Responses: accept, buck, comply, cry out, encourage, heave, jerk, moan, open, pant, part, recoil, respond, go rigid, resist, scream, sigh, snort, slither, stiffen, struggle, sob, squeal, squirm, struggle, surrender, thrash, thresh, twist, whimper, wiggle, wriggle, writhe, yelp, yield.

Pleasure: bliss, delectation, delight, delirium, ecstasy, elation, enjoyment, enraptured, enticing, euphoria, exquisite, exultation, fervor, frenzy, gratification, joy, luscious, lush, rapture, rich, satisfaction, savor, tempting, transport, wild.

Torso: abdomen, abs, back, belly, bellybutton, buttocks, chest, collarbone, flank, gut, kidneys, middle, midriff, navel, paunch, rib cage, ribs, scapula, shoulder-blade, shoulder, six-pack, spine, small of the back, sternum, solar plexus, stomach, tummy, vertebra.

Secretions: ambrosia, bubbling, cum, damp, drenched, dripping, ejaculate, emission, jism, juicy, love juice, luscious, lush, melted, moist, nectar, oozing, perspiration, pre-cum, saliva, sap, secretion, semen, soaked, sodden, sperm, spittle, succulent, sweat, tears, viscous, volcano, wet.

Sexual Intercourse: bonk, bugger, consummate, couple, enter, fornicate, frig, fuck, get laid, grind, hump, lie with, make love, make out, mount, nail, penetrate, plow/plough, pump, ride, rut, roger, score, screw, service, shag, take, tumble, violate; anilingus, blow job, cunnilingus, eat [pussy], fellatio, give head, gobble, go down, lip service, muff diving, rim job, rimming, sixty-nine, sucking, tipping the velvet.

Virginity: chastity, chasteness, cherry, hymen, innocence, maidenhead, modesty, purity, unsullied, untouched, virgin, virtue.

Appendix D
On-line Resources for Erotica Writers

This appendix lists a selection of web resources for erotica writers seeking exposure, market data, discussion and feedback, independent publication, or general information on the genre.

- **Erotica-Readers.com**
  This is the one to visit for up-to-date market information; click through *Author Resources* to the *Calls for Submissions* page where you will find contact information and links to submission guidelines for a several dozen erotic markets. Also features book reviews, an email discussion list, and much more.

- **asstr.org**
  A story repository for the alt.sex.stories Usenet newsgroup. Here you can create a free author's web site, archive your erotic fiction, and make it available via (non-commercial) online publication.

- **Literotica.com**
  A website promoting and collecting erotic literature. Also maintains an archive of articles on erotic writing. Accepts user submissions, holds competitions, and publishes an occasional print anthology called the *Literotica Book.*

- **EroticAuthorsAssociation.com**
  This membership-based site is aimed at erotica professionals (including authors who have self-published or who have been published electronically). Includes a market-oriented blog.

- **EroticFiction.Tribe.net**
  A web-based forum for readers and writers of erotic fiction to share stories, feedback, and discussion.

- **lulu.com**
  Lulu's lack of up-front fees makes it one of the best and lowest-risk places for aspiring independent POD publishers to start, but don't expect it to make you rich or famous.

About the Author

In the early 1990s, Han Li Thorn gave up his software engineering day job to embark on a career as a freelance writer, instructor and training consultant. He began writing novel-length erotica at the turn of the millennium; in 2003 he turned down interest from one of the trade majors in favor of the greater control and long-term potential of electronic and on-demand publication.

Published works:

Spike Trap
Property Rites
Rough Copy

(writing as Huw Lyan Thomas)

Better than Real

Printed in the United Kingdom by
Lightning Source UK Ltd., Milton Keynes
142322UK00001B/167/A